THE LIBRARY OF
AMERICAN
LIVES AND TIMES™

OLIVER WENDELL HOLMES JR.

The Supreme Court and American Legal Thought

Sophie W. Littlefield
William M. Wiecek

The Rosen Publishing Group's
PowerPlus Books™
New York

For Tyler and Sally Anne, our family's youngest readers

Published in 2005 by The Rosen Publishing Group, Inc.
29 East 21st Street, New York, NY 10010

First Edition

Editor's Note: All quotations have been reproduced as they appeared in the letters and diaries from which they were borrowed. No correction was made to the inconsistent spelling that was common in that time period.

Library of Congress Cataloging-in-Publication Data

Littlefield, Sophie W.
Oliver Wendell Holmes Jr. : the Supreme Court and American legal thought / Sophie W. Littlefield, William M. Wiecek.
     p. cm.
Includes bibliographical references and index.
Contents: Growing up in Boston — Serving in the Civil war — A young lawyer and the common law — Becoming a judge — An appointment to the United States Supreme Court — "Fundamental principles . . . of our people and our law" — Congress and child labor — Free speech and the First Amendment — World War I changes everything — Final years.
ISBN 1-4042-2652-4 (library binding)
1. Holmes, Oliver Wendell, 1809–1894. 2. Judges—United States—Biography—Juvenile literature. 3. United States. Supreme Court—Officials and employees—Biography—Juvenile literature. [1. Holmes, Oliver Wendell, 1809–1894. 2. Judges. 3. United States. Supreme Court.] I. Title: Oliver Wendell Holmes Jr. II. Wiecek, William M., 1938– III. Title.
KF8745.H6L58 2005
347.73'2634—dc21

                    2003010715

Manufactured in the United States of America

CONTENTS

Introduction 5

1. Growing Up in Boston 8

2. Serving in the Civil War .21

3. A Young Lawyer and *The Common Law* 32

4. Becoming a Judge 39

5. An Appointment to the United States Supreme Court . . .51

6. "Fundamental Principles" 62

7. Congress and Child Labor 70

8. Free Speech and the First Amendment 79

9. World War I Changes Everything 84

10. Final Years 92

Timeline 100
Glossary 102
Additional Resources 105
Bibliography 106
Index 107
About the Authors 109
Primary Sources 110
Credits 112

Introduction

Oliver Wendell Holmes Jr., the most famous American judge of the twentieth century, enjoyed a long, successful life. He was born in 1841, and he died in 1935, at the age of ninety-three. A graduate of Harvard College and a veteran of the Civil War, Holmes began his study of law in 1864. He went on to write or edit some of the most influential legal books, articles, and journals of his time. He was appointed to the Supreme Judicial Court of Massachusetts at the age of 41, which is young to be a justice. He sat on its bench for two decades and became the court's chief justice in 1899. Eager to rise higher in the ranks of the American judiciary, Holmes set his sights on the U.S. Supreme Court. He got his wish in 1902, when President Theodore Roosevelt nominated him to the nation's highest court. Holmes served there for thirty years. In those three decades, he wrote opinions that defined the way Americans thought about

Opposite: This photograph of Oliver Wendell Holmes was taken in 1910. At that time, he had sat on the U.S. Supreme Court for about eight years. When he retired in 1932, at age 90, he was the oldest justice ever to have served on the U.S. Supreme Court.

The U.S. Constitution was written in 1787 and was ratified, or put into effect, two years later. The Constitution is the United States' supreme law. All statutes, court decisions, and acts of government throughout the United States must follow it. The Constitution protects the rights of the American people. It requires state and federal governments to serve and protect the people. After an introduction, called the Preamble, the main body of the Constitution defines how the government is structured and how changes can be made to the Constitution itself.

Twenty-seven amendments, or changes, have been made to the Constitution. These amendments are now part of the Constitution. The first ten were adopted in 1791. Together they are known as the Bill of Rights. The most recent amendment was made in 1992.

law throughout the twentieth century. Many of those opinions were dissents, which means he disagreed with decisions reached by a majority of the court.

The U.S. Supreme Court plays an important role in American life, even though it has no political power of its own. The justices cannot make laws. They do not command armies or police, and they cannot tax citizens or spend federal funds. Their authority comes from the power of their ideas. Their job is to decide cases, which can change how the U.S. Constitution is interpreted. By doing so the Supreme Court controls the development of American law. This awesome power is called judicial review. The court has the power to decide that a statute enacted by the U.S. Congress or a state legislature violates the Constitution and therefore must not be enforced. It can also decide that the actions of the president, other federal officials, or state officials have violated the Constitution and declare their acts void.

Holmes made important contributions to the development of American law during his time on the Supreme Court. He introduced ideas about how systems of law work and why people should be held responsible for their actions. These ideas continue to influence the way Supreme Court cases are decided. More than any other American judge, Holmes influenced the development of modern law.

1. Growing Up in Boston

Oliver Wendell Holmes Jr.'s ancestors settled in Massachusetts before the American Revolution. There they became leaders in business, politics, and religion. They built homes in and around the growing town of Boston and filled them with furniture and paintings brought from England. They employed servants, traveled in fine horse-drawn carriages, and dressed in clothing modeled on European designs. They valued education and sent their children to private grammar schools and then to Harvard College or Yale College.

Holmes's father, Oliver Wendell

Franz Xavier Habermann created this hand-colored engraving, entitled *View of the Town Hall, Boston,* just after the American Revolution. In the late eighteenth century, Boston was the intellectual and cultural center of the United States.

Holmes Sr., was born in Cambridge, Massachusetts, to the Reverend Abiel Holmes and his wife, Amelia. He was an active child who rebelled against the silence and strict rules of the household, despite severe punishments. He liked to read and to write poetry. After attending Harvard College, Holmes Sr. studied medicine in Paris, France, and then returned to Boston to practice and teach at the Harvard Medical School. Dr. Holmes soon returned to his writing and published poetry and essays that were widely admired. He was invited to give lectures on such diverse topics as travel,

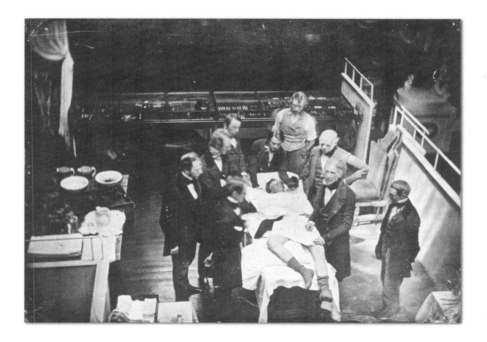

This photograph of Doctor Oliver Wendell Holmes was taken in 1846. The patient on the table has been rendered unconscious by a drug called ether, the use of which was a recent development. The patient is being operated on by Dr. John Collins.

The USS *Constitution* earned the nickname Old Ironsides during the War of 1812. Legend has it that, during a battle, shots fired from the British ship *Guerrière* failed to penetrate the oak sides of the *Constitution*.

The poem "Old Ironsides" made Dr. Holmes famous. It celebrates the famous warship known by that nickname. When Dr. Holmes heard that the U.S. Navy planned to scuttle, or sink, the venerable old ship in 1830, he wrote the poem in angry, sarcastic protest. Thanks in part to his poetic indignation, the navy saved the ship from destruction. Old Ironsides still floats in Boston Harbor.

poetry, France, and medicine. The income he received from these lectures, combined with his salary from Harvard, provided a comfortable living.

In 1840, Dr. Holmes married Amelia Jackson. Her father, Charles Jackson, was a wealthy judge who had served on the Supreme Judicial Court of Massachusetts. The Jacksons presented the newlyweds with a large, stately house in the Beacon Hill neighborhood of Boston. The Holmeses were happy in their new home. They lived among the social elite. Amelia was a devoted wife, and Holmes enjoyed his work. One year after their wedding, Oliver Wendell Holmes Jr. was born. A sister, named Amelia for her mother, followed two years later. A

This photo of Holmes's mother, Amelia Lee Jackson Holmes, was taken in 1875, when she was fifty-seven years old. She described herself as a dedicated mother, even writing to her son in 1866, "I assure you that I give more thoughts to [my children] than to anything else in the world."

This photograph of the Holmes children was taken in 1855. From left to right are Edward (age 9), Amelia (age 11), and Oliver (age 14). The Holmes children, especially Oliver, the eldest, were raised with high expectations to succeed. Oliver was sometimes irritated by what he felt was Dr. Holmes's tendency to be highly critical of his children.

brother, named Edward and nicknamed Ned, was born in 1846.

In the early decades of the nineteenth century, the face of Boston was changing. When Oliver Wendell Holmes Jr. was born, Boston still felt like a small town. In the words of his friend Henry Cabot Lodge, who grew up nearby, "Boston itself was then small enough to be satisfying to a boy's desires. It was possible to grasp one's little world and to know and to be known by everybody in one's own fragment of society."

The "little world" Lodge described was a lovely one. Beacon Hill was filled with large, stone houses and elegant brick row houses. The marshy waters of the nearby Back Bay brought salty breezes through the streets of town.

This small-town feeling changed dramatically as immigrants from around the world arrived in greater numbers and settled near Holmes's seaside neighborhood. In the 1840s alone, some thirty thousand Irish Catholic immigrants arrived and settled in and around the small city. Italian, German, French Canadian, Polish, Lithuanian, Portuguese, and Chinese settlers also came to stay. By the time Holmes was a young man, more than half of the residents of Boston had emigrated from other lands.

Holmes's father noted the changes around them. Dr. Holmes was something of a snob. He said a person from New England would feel more among "his own people" in London "than in one of our seaboard cities." He compared his own society to that of Indian royalty. At the time, the highest level of India's caste system was the Brahmin caste, so Holmes used the phrase to describe his fellow prosperous and influential New Englanders. Later the term was shortened to Brahmins or Boston Brahmins. Brahmin society included some of the wealthiest residents of Boston. They valued hard work and prayer, but they also enjoyed literature, poetry, and the politics of the growing city around them.

Young Holmes, known as Wendie among family and later as Wendell among friends, was educated alongside other privileged Boston children. The Holmes household enjoyed lively conversation between father and children. At the dinner table, everyone talked at once, and, if the children were especially clever, their father rewarded them with marmalade. These mealtime conversations inspired Dr. Holmes to write a series of magazine essays in which a fictional narrator, seated at the breakfast table of a rooming house, muses about current events. Dr. Holmes titled this series The Autocrat of the Breakfast Table. An autocrat is someone with influence and power, and Dr. Holmes enjoyed his influence in his own dining room and later with his many readers. The Autocrat became a friendly nickname for Dr. Holmes on his lecture tours.

Dr. Holmes enjoyed engaging his children in debate, but he did not like to lose. He pushed the conversation to the point of competition, especially with his bright eldest son. Dr. Holmes and young Wendie were often locked in debate and stubborn disagreement. Father and son loved each other, but they rarely showed it. Overcoming Dr. Holmes's literary success would become a lifelong challenge to his son. Wendie would spend his life trying to assert his identity beyond the shadow of his famous father. He hated being known merely as "the son of Dr. Holmes" and struggled to create his own reputation.

The Autocrat of the Breakfast Table, a caricature of Oliver Wendell Holmes Sr., was created by Spy, the pseudonym of Leslie Matthew Ward (1851–1922), for the June 19, 1886, issue of *Vanity Fair* magazine.

On the other hand, Wendie's mother, Amelia, showered her son with love and encouragement. At that time, few women received a formal education. Most were expected to spend their time and energy running the household. A devoted wife and mother, Amelia supported her husband and children in every way, tending to their comfort and offering them praise. Though Amelia rarely expressed opinions of her own, on one subject she was firm. She believed that slavery was wrong and that Americans must stop keeping slaves. Amelia was an abolitionist, or someone who fought to abolish the institution of slavery. By 1804, all states north of Maryland had abolished slavery within their borders, but this legislation had no effect on the stronghold of slavery, the American South. Slavery was the foundation of the economic and social framework of the South, and, by the 1830s, the South's cotton-based agriculture was crucial to national industries. Northerners as well as southerners resisted the total emancipation of slaves, but American abolitionists continued the fight, and the debate grew more heated through the 1840s and 1850s. Many northerners hoped for a peaceful and lawful solution to the question of slavery. Other abolitionists, especially in Boston, believed that ending slavery was more important than preserving the union of the states. They were prepared to go to war.

In the fall of 1857, Wendie Holmes had other things on his mind. At the age of sixteen, he was about to leave home to attend Harvard College. Today Harvard's campus is known around the world, and it attracts top students and scholars. In Holmes's time, however, it was just a few brick buildings surrounding a muddy yard. There were fewer than one hundred students in Holmes's class. The dormitories were drafty. Students drew their water from a well in the yard. The college day began with religious services in chapel, and classes continued until nine o'clock in the evening. When called on by a teacher, students were expected to stand and recite the ancient history, Latin, and Greek that they had learned the day before, or answer questions about their mathematics, rhetoric, English literature, and science lessons. This kind of education, based on memorization and drill, bored Holmes. Only science held any interest for him. He found the scientific methods of observation and analysis powerfully convincing. He loved to detect patterns in collections of data. He would later use these same scientific methods as no one had done before, to study history. He would draw insights into the development of law from a scientific study of his-

This photograph of Holmes as an undergraduate at Harvard was taken in about 1859.

Patrick School
Washington, IL

This lithograph poster advertises *Scribner's* magazine, which featured an article about student life at Harvard. Although he was sometimes bored with his studies, Holmes described the social life at Harvard as a "perfect delight."

tory.

Holmes had a full social life at Harvard. He enjoyed mingling with young women and had no trouble attracting them. He joined the Porcellian Club and the Hasty Pudding Club. The activities of these social clubs revolved around dining, reciting poetry, performing silly plays, and singing late into the evening. Norwood Penrose Hallowell, nicknamed Pen, was also a member of the Hasty Pudding Club. Hallowell was a fiery abolitionist, and his dedication to the cause inspired Holmes. The two men became great friends. When Hallowell died after the war, Holmes called him "the most generously gallant spirit and I don't know but the greatest soul I ever knew."

The students and profes-

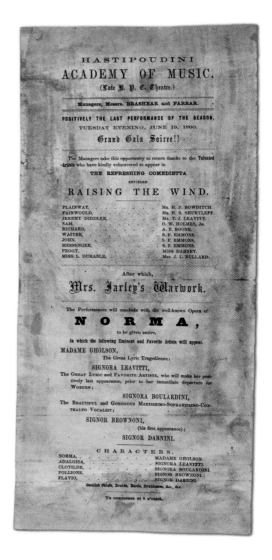

Harvard's Hasty Pudding Club began as a secret society in 1795. When Holmes was a member, the club had begun to produce student-written shows. The club also performed operas and contemporary plays, and held mock trials. In this program, Holmes is credited as "O.W. Holmes, Jr."

sors at Harvard tried to ignore the threats of war that sounded beyond their campus, but the regimental drumbeat was growing louder. In the fall of Holmes's senior year, Republican candidate Abraham Lincoln was elected president of the United States. Certain that Lincoln and the Republican Party meant to outlaw slavery entirely, eleven southern states seceded from the Union and formed the Confederate States of America. In April, Confederate forces fired on federal troops at Fort Sumter, and the Civil War began. In the spring of 1861, inspired by Pen Hallowell, Holmes joined the Fourth Battalion of Massachusetts Volunteers as a private. In August of that year, he received a commission as a first lieutenant for the Twentieth Massachusetts Volunteer Infantry Regiment of the New England Guard. He left Harvard, aware that, in doing so, he might be giving up the right to graduate with his classmates. When Holmes announced his plans to enlist, his father tried to discourage him, but his mother wrote to a friend, "I only hope and pray that the war may go on till every slave is free, and that my child will always be ready to defend and struggle for humanity." As it turned out, Harvard permitted Holmes to take his final exams and receive his degree before he left for active service. When he fought his first Civil War battles, he did so as a fresh young graduate of Harvard College.

2. Serving in the Civil War

Oliver Wendell Holmes Jr. had a romantic notion of war. War was a gentleman's pursuit, at least for officers such as himself. The pursuit of personal honor was as important as the fight for political, social, or moral aims. Slavery had corrupted the South, and Holmes and many of his classmates believed it was their duty to reform civilization, just as warriors had done since the Middle Ages. Holmes also sought adventure, excitement, and the opportunity to prove his bravery. Much later, Holmes would write, "Through our great good fortune, in our youth our hearts were touched with fire." Without this early passion, Holmes and his fellow soldiers could not have met the physical and emotional demands of combat.

This photo of Holmes was taken in 1861, the first year of his service in the Civil War.

In September, Holmes traveled to Maryland with the 750-man Twentieth Massachusetts Regiment. He began in good spirits. The soldiers spent most of their time drilling, or practicing fighting formations until the movements came easily. The food was not very good, and the men slept twelve to a room, but Holmes was at ease and, as he wrote in a letter to his mother, did not expect to encounter combat soon. The regiment maneuvered along the Potomac River, the boundary between Maryland and Virginia, and between the Northern and Southern armies, observing

The design of the battle flag of the Twentieth Massachusetts Regiment is derived from Massachusetts's seal. The banner shows the state's motto in Latin: *Ense petit placidam sub libertate quietem,* which means "By the sword we seek peace, but peace only under liberty."

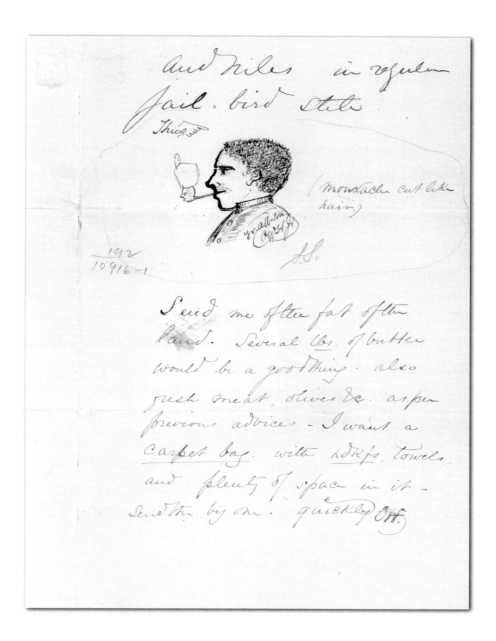

Holmes wrote this letter to his mother in May 1861, while he was at Fort Independence on Castle Island, Massachusetts. In the letter he says that he is in "bully [good] condition." He included a self-portrait to show off his new haircut and mustache.

Confederate forces on the opposite riverbank and preparing to engage the enemy. Then, on October 20, the Twentieth Massachusetts was ordered to cross the river into Virginia.

By the afternoon of October 21, the Twentieth Massachusetts found themselves exposed and surrounded by Confederates. They stood in a field at the top of a 150-foot (45.7-m) cliff known as Ball's Bluff. The river lay below, and Confederate troops hid in the surrounding woods. After the dull security of the parade ground, Holmes and his fellow soldiers would finally confront the realities of war. They quickly lost their idealism. The Confederates attacked, and more than half of the Union soldiers were captured, killed, or wounded. Holmes was one of them. He was shot in the chest during the final hours of the battle.

Camp life and combat during the Civil War was often brutal. Union and Confederate soldiers slept in the open on hard ground. Food, if it was available at all, was simple. There were no radios. Scouts on horseback relayed combat information. Battlefield commanders led their men into battle with little information about the enemy or the terrain. Infantrymen carried muskets, which frequently jammed. Soldiers advanced through the thick smoke of musket fire and the thunder of cannons, and fell wounded and dead in great numbers. Medical facilities and supplies were simple and scarce. Deadly diseases, such as dysentery, typhoid, and malaria, were common. More soldiers died of disease than from battle wounds. Doctors amputated arms or legs in the field with crude, dirty saws and nothing except whiskey to ease the soldiers' pain. The dead were often left for days on the field, where they became prey for scavenging animals. Eventually they were buried in mass graves.

The minié ball that struck Holmes in the chest at Ball's Bluff missed all his vital organs. After he was rescued from the battleground, Holmes spent several days in a field hospital. Then he traveled home to Boston to recover and rest. He returned to the front the next spring.

This stereograph of a Civil War field hospital was created in 1862. Stereographs are two pictures that are taken side-by-side and from slightly different angles, which, when viewed through a device called a stereoscope, produce a three-dimensional image.

By March 1862, Holmes and the rest of the Army of the Potomac had advanced into Virginia and were encamped near Hampton. The Army of the Potomac was on the march to Richmond, Virginia, with plans to capture the Confederate capital and deliver a decisive blow to the Confederate cause. Confederate general Robert E. Lee was determined to thwart the Union army's advance. On June 25, Lee's troops attacked. The ensuing struggle, known as the Seven Days' Battle, dragged on until the Union's heavy losses led the soldiers to withdraw. Even in retreat, the bloodshed continued. Holmes's regiment marched through the night and fought every afternoon. They had almost nothing to eat or drink.

The Union forces continued their march north, finally regrouping near Washington, D.C. Lee, buoyed by the recent victory, decided to send his troops into Union territory. The Confederate troops gathered in Keedysville, just north of the Potomac River, near Sharpsburg, Maryland. The Union army advanced on the Confederate forces, and, on September 17, 1862, Holmes and the Twentieth Massachusetts faced Confederate troops in the Battle of Antietam. This was one of the bloodiest battles of the entire war. Holmes was shot in back of the neck, but the wound was not life-threatening. He returned home to Boston, but after less than two months' convalescence there, he rejoined his regiment in Virginia.

Encouraged by the Union victory at Antietam, President Abraham Lincoln issued a preliminary version of the Emancipation Proclamation in September 1862. This document declared that all slaves in the Confederate states would be emancipated, or freed, by the U.S. government if the Confederacy did not end its rebellion by January 1 of the coming year. The proclamation did not free the slaves in states that had remained loyal to the Union, however. As such, it was a cautious document, and it had no concrete effects. Yet the message was clear. The war's purpose had changed. The North was fighting not only to save the Union, but also to abolish slavery.

On September 17, 1862, Lieutenant Colonel William LeDuc sent a telegram to Holmes's family to notify them of their son's injury. It reads: "Capt Holmes wounded, shot through the neck. Thought not mortal at Keedysville [Antietam]."

Oliver Wendell Holmes Jr. had changed as well. In Virginia, the men of the Twentieth Massachusetts had lost heart. There would not be the quick and certain

Following spread: The Battle of Chancellorsville, where Holmes was wounded for the third time, lasted from May 1 through May 5, 1863. The casualties were high for this battle. The Union lost seventeen thousand soldiers, while the Confederates lost twelve thousand.

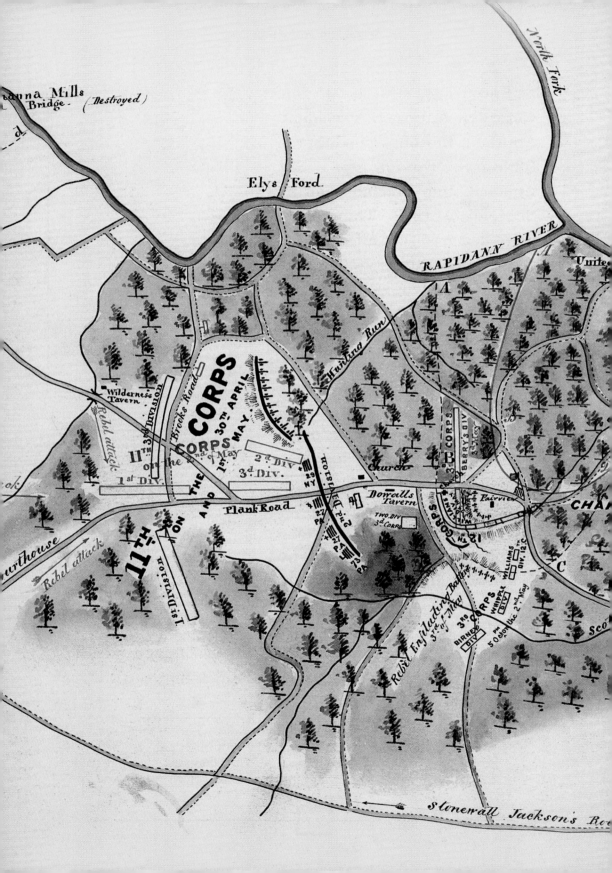

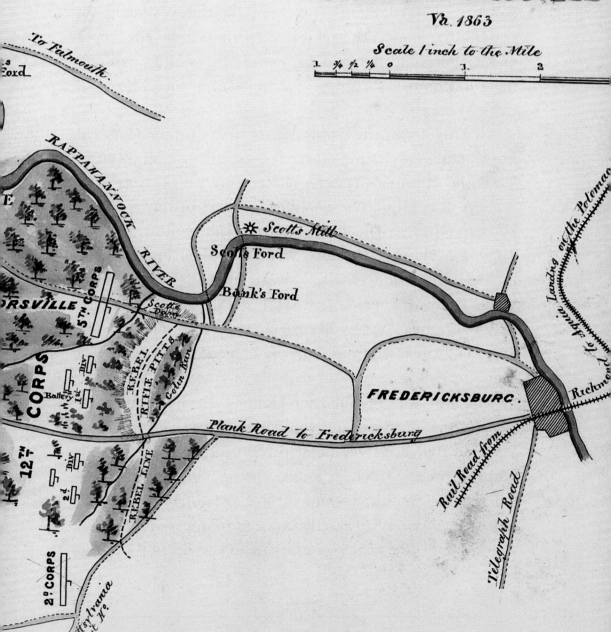

Map
of the Battlefield of
CHANCELLORSVILLE
Va. 1863

Scale 1 inch to the Mile

1 ¾ ½ ¼ 0 1 2

To Falmouth.

Ford.

RAPPAHANNOCK RIVER

Scotts Mill

Scotts Ford

Bank's Ford

5TH CORPS

...RSVILLE

Scotts Dam

REBEL RIFLE PITTS

Colin Run

FREDERICKSBURG.

Richmond

To Aquia Landing on the Potomac

CORPS

Div. 1st.

Battery

Div. 2d.

12TH

Plank Road to Fredericksburg

Rail Road from

REBEL LINE

Telegraph Road

2d CORPS

To Spottsylvania Court Ho.

victory for which they had hoped. Holmes had given up his romantic notions of saving the South from the corruption of slavery, and he had shed his illusions about battle. He had become pessimistic about the outcome of the war. "I see no further progress—I don't think . . . you realize the unity or the determination of the South," he wrote in a letter to his father. The Army of the Potomac decided to spend the winter camped near Falmouth, Virginia, and to resume the campaign in the spring.

In May 1863, the Confederate army under General Lee attacked Union forces near Chancellorsville, Virginia. Holmes's regiment stood by to the rear as a reserve force, but Holmes was not out of harm's way. He was shot in the heel. At first the wound did not appear serious, but there were complications, and it took Holmes more than seven months to recover. Exhausted and weakened, Holmes decided he would leave the army when his term of service was up. On July 17, 1864, Holmes was discharged. He returned home to Boston.

The war was finished for Holmes. He had fought in some of the bloodiest, most important battles of the Civil War. He had been wounded three times and each time had returned to the field as soon as he had been able. He felt that he could not endure the hardships of the front line any longer. With the distance of many years, Homes would recall the war as a glorious experience. "As life is action and passion, it is required of a man that he should share the passion and action of his time at peril of being judged not to have lived," he said in an 1884 Memorial Day speech. In 1864, however, the war-weary, wounded, discouraged veteran wanted only to go home to Boston and begin his life anew. As he wrote his mother just before his term of service ended, he had "started in this thing a boy [but] I am now a man."

3. A Young Lawyer and *The Common Law*

In the fall of 1864, Oliver Wendell Holmes Jr. entered Harvard Law School. Just two years later, he received his degree and began to work for the law firm of George Shattuck, where Holmes would spend nearly all of the next two decades before his appointment to the Supreme Judicial Court of Massachusetts.

During law school and the first few years of law practice, Holmes lived at his family's home. He spent time with friends his age, all members of New England's elite society. Among Holmes's young female friends was Fanny Dixwell, whom he had known since childhood. They had written to each other while Holmes was at war. Holmes's parents liked Fanny and were impressed with her intelligence. His father called her "a young lady of most remarkable gifts and qualities." Holmes must have agreed, because he proposed to Fanny in March 1872. They were both thirty-one years old. They were married that June in Old North Church in Boston.

When Holmes began his career in the law, he and Fanny did not have much money. Fanny came to live with

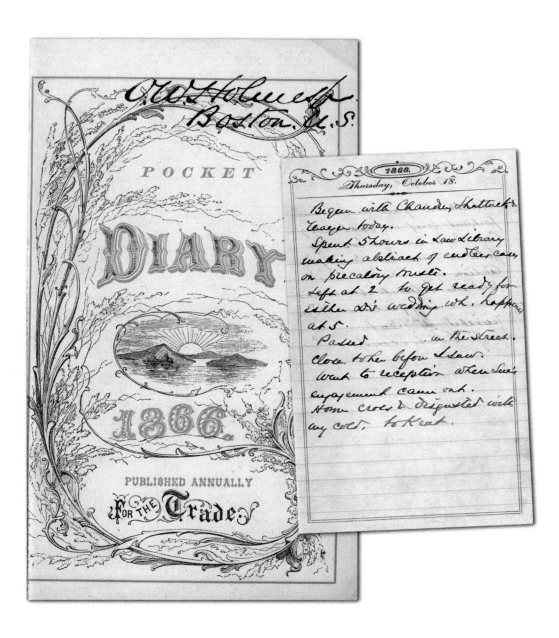

Holmes kept a diary throughout his life. This is his 1866 journal.
Inset: On October 18 of that year, he wrote of his starting at George
Shattuck's law firm. He wrote that he spent "5 hours at the law
library" before leaving at 2:00 P.M. to get ready for a wedding that
began at 5:00 P.M.

Fanny Dixwell married Holmes in 1872. Soon after the wedding, she contracted an illness called rheumatic fever, which left her bedridden for several months and made her sick again many years later. This photograph was taken in 1860, when she was 20 years old.

Holmes at his parents' home. Fanny understood the demands of Holmes's career, however, and was prepared to support him, despite his long hours at work. She was a solitary person and did not care to entertain visitors. While Holmes immersed himself in his work, she kept herself busy with embroidering, caring for her pets, and running the household. When they were together, Fanny and Holmes were affectionate with each other. Fanny read to Holmes in the evenings, teased him when he grew too serious, and supported him however she could.

It was common at the time for young, educated people to travel to Europe if they could afford it. Holmes had enjoyed visiting England as a single man, and he returned every few years after his wedding. Fanny did not like to travel and usually stayed at home. When in London, Holmes did not work or study, but rather filled his days with social visits and parties, activities he did not have time for at home.

As an increasingly important figure at George Shattuck's firm, Holmes began to represent companies in business disputes. He specialized in a branch of the law that dealt with maritime commerce. These cases provided him and Fanny with a comfortable living. They were able to get an apartment in Boston and a country house in rural Mattapoisett, Massachusetts, where they spent long weekends. However, in time Holmes grew bored with the day-to-day law practice. "I wish that the necessity of making a living didn't preclude any choice on my part," he wrote in August 1879, "for I hate business and dislike practice apart from arguing cases."

Partly to escape the monotony of casework, Holmes dedicated many long hours to legal scholarship. He carefully studied the development of law through history and in different cultures, considered the way new laws were made, and began to develop his own ideas about how law should develop in the future. Holmes admired the scientific method of organizing facts, and he tried to

This photograph was taken in October 1872, about three months after Holmes's marriage to Fanny. At that time he was practicing law in Boston and editing the *American Law Review*.

structure his thoughts in a similar fashion. The history of law was "a thick fog of details—in a black and frozen night," he would write later, and the work was difficult. Holmes was not paid for this private scholarship, but he sought more than a large income. He wanted to create something new and significant that would improve the way the legal system worked and that also would establish his place in history. Because he was challenging accepted beliefs, Holmes chose to work alone, even though he was not a loner by nature. "No one," he wrote, "can cut out new paths in company. He does that alone." Colleagues and friends admired his dedication. One friend insisted that Holmes "knows more law than anyone in Boston of our time, and works harder at it than anyone."

In the fall of 1880, while preparing a series of lectures for Boston University, Holmes realized that he had collected enough material for a book. In March 1881, Holmes published that book, titled *The Common Law*. It is considered among the best books ever written about law.

Few scholars had ever made such a thorough study of the way law had evolved over the course of a people's history. Holmes investigated how legal codes had developed in primitive societies and in ancient Rome and Europe. Holmes wrote in *The Common Law*, "The law embodies the story of a nation's development through many centuries." As such, law reflects the moral and social development of the people it governs. Law, he reasoned, could be defined very simply as "the prophecies of what the courts will do." Holmes explained that "it is the merit of the common law that it decides the

344   THE COMMON LAW.

as B could show no title, he could readily maintain under the fiction that he was the same person as A, whose title was not denied.

It is not necessary at this point to study family rights in the German tribes. For it is not disputed that the modern executor derives his characteristics from the Roman heir. Wills also were borrowed from Rome, and were unknown to the Germans of Tacitus.[1] Administrators were a later imitation of executors, introduced by statute for cases where there was no will, or where, for any other reason, executors were wanting. The executor has the legal title to the whole of the testator's personal estate, and, generally speaking, the power of alienation. Formerly he was entitled to the undistrib-

The Common Law was published in 1881. On the page shown, Holmes wrote notes in the margins in preparation for his lectures.

case first and determines the principle afterwards." He believed that judges should resolve legal problems by the "objective method." Judges should not try to guess what was on a person's mind at the time he or she committed an act. Rather, he said, law should be based on what reasonable persons would do in the same situation.

The Common Law was well received by Holmes's colleagues, but it was not widely read, and it did not earn him the scholarly reputation he hoped for. He was disappointed further to be passed over twice, in 1881 and again in 1882, for a position on the Supreme Judicial Court of Massachusetts. For a time, it seemed as though he would never be appointed to that court. Early in 1882, with no other way to escape the daily practice of law, he accepted a professorship at Harvard Law School. He and Fanny traveled to Europe for the summer, and, when they returned, Holmes began to teach courses in constitutional law and jurisprudence. Though most people would have been satisfied with a career of private practice capped by an appointment to the Harvard Law School faculty, Holmes wanted more. He was ambitious and aware of his remarkable talents. He believed that being a law professor removed him from "the practical struggle of life" and was "the less manly course." The school year had barely begun, however, when an unexpected event changed the course of his future.

4. Becoming a Judge

When he had agreed to teach at Harvard, Oliver Wendell Holmes Jr. had insisted that he be free to consider the offer of a judgeship. Such an offer came suddenly and unexpectedly after Holmes had been teaching for only three months. In the fall of 1882, one of the judges of the Supreme Judicial Court of Massachusetts became ill and announced his plans to retire. The responsibility of naming a replacement fell to the governor of Massachusetts. He chose Holmes, a respected lawyer, author, and law professor.

George Shattuck delivered the governor's offer to Holmes while Holmes was eating lunch. "It was a stroke of lightning," Shattuck later said. The Governor's Council, which had to approve the nomination, was meeting that very afternoon at three o'clock to consider the appointment, so Holmes could not delay his decision. Holmes accepted the position and abruptly left teaching. His speedy departure annoyed his colleagues at Harvard, who did not agree with Holmes that teaching "is but half life." Dr. Holmes reacted to the honor bestowed on his son

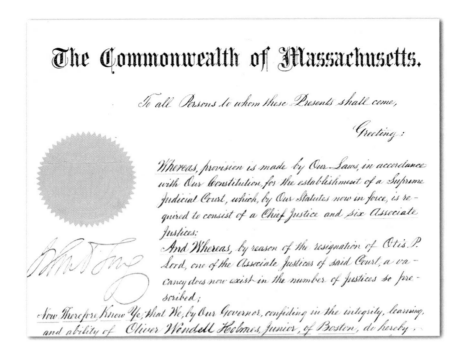

The Commonwealth of Massachusetts.

To all Persons to whom these Presents shall come,

Greeting:

Whereas, provision is made by Our Laws, in accordance with Our Constitution, for the establishment of a Supreme Judicial Court, which, by Our Statutes now in force, is required to consist of a Chief Justice and six Associate Justices:

And Whereas, by reason of the resignation of Otis P. Lord, one of the Associate Justices of said Court, a vacancy does now exist in the number of Justices so prescribed;

Now Therefore, Know Ye, that We, by Our Governor, confiding in the integrity, learning, and ability of Oliver Wendell Holmes, junior, of Boston, do hereby .

This is the announcement of Holmes's appointment to the Supreme Judicial Court of Massachusetts. His departure from Harvard angered many of his colleagues, but, as William Weld observed, "as he expressly reserved the right to accept a judgeship, we cannot complain."

with a wry smile: "To think of it—my little boy a judge, and able to send me to jail if I don't behave myself." Holmes took his seat on the Supreme Judicial Court when he was forty-one years old, and he would serve there for twenty years. The lifestyle enjoyed by Holmes and Fanny Holmes soon changed. With his judge's salary, the couple bought a home at the foot of the fashionable Beacon Hill neighborhood. While Fanny attended to the details of furnishing and staffing the house, Holmes immersed himself in his new job.

The Supreme Judicial Court, Massachusetts's highest court, did both trial and appellate work. These are the two kinds of courts. Trial courts hear the trials of cases, in which lawyers introduce evidence and question witnesses. If someone is unhappy with the result of a decision in a trial court, that person can appeal the decision to a higher court, which is called an appellate court. The appellate court decides either that the trial result was correct and affirms the trial court's decision, or that it was wrong as a matter of law. Then it reverses the decision and can send the case back to be tried again. Today only the most important cases go to the highest court of the state. At the time Holmes sat on the state court, though, the judges heard disputes between neighbors and families, tried local crimes, and worked on the small, everyday details of the law. Massachusetts's citizens sued over business disputes, divorce, injuries from accidents, and arguments that ended in violence. Holmes and his fellow judges had to decide all these cases both in trials and on appeal.

During the summer, the justices of the Supreme Judicial Court of Massachusetts traveled throughout different parts of the state to hear cases. In the fall, winter, and spring, the seven justices sat together in Boston to hear appeals. Holmes discovered that traveling the circuit of county courthouses was hard work. He hoped that he would be able to meet the physical

This photograph of the judges of the Supreme Judicial Court of Massachusetts was taken between 1899 and 1902, while Holmes was chief justice. From left to right are pictured John Wilkes Hammond, John Lohtrop, Marcus Perrin Knowlton, Oliver Wendell Holmes Jr., James Madison Morton, William Caleb Loring.

challenges of the job. He recalled that his grandfather, a judge, had resigned because of overwork. At the county courts, the judges sat on hard wooden benches and wore stiff, formal clothing. Such exhausting work put an end to Holmes's social life. "I can't [dine out] and feel as well and fit for work the next day," he remarked. When traveling on circuit, he dined alone in his room after a long day at court because Fanny did not travel with him. They made up for these lonely evenings apart by spending weekends together at their summer home on the coast.

At first, Holmes was excited about his work. It was "most valuable for an all round view of the law," he wrote an English friend shortly after he began his work as a judge. "One sees too a good deal of human nature & I find that I am interested all the time." Early on he enthused, "I enjoy the work so far extremely." Holmes took great satisfaction in doing it well, writing that "The joy of life is to put out one's power in some natural and useful . . . way." He enjoyed "the pure pleasure of doing the work." However, as time went on, Holmes lost some of his enthusiasm for his work, especially the hard, lonely trial work of the summer months. He came to believe that most of the cases coming before his court on appeal were not very important, measured either by the question of law involved or by the number of people affected. "No very great or burning questions have been before me" he concluded after ten years' service on the Supreme Judicial Court. In 1900, while speaking to a group of Bostonian lawyers, Holmes considered his career as a judge and realized that he had decided nearly one thousand cases. "Many of them," he said, were "on trifling or transitory matters." He concluded, "Alas, gentlemen, that is life."

One of these cases concerned a man who was using an outhouse, or an outdoor toilet, in a shed located on railroad company property when a train jumped the track, struck the outhouse, and killed him. Could his

This is a postcard from about 1910 of the Holmes's summer home in Beverly Farms, Massachusetts. Holmes often mockingly referred to the estate as "Beverly-by-the-Depot."

heirs recover damages for his wrongful death? Holmes held that they could not, because the man was a trespasser, someone who did not have a legal right to be on the property of another. The deceased took the risk of unlawfully being on the railroad's property, so the railroad was not responsible for any injuries that he sustained there.

Another appellate case concerned a man who left his horse tied up near a public sidewalk. The horse kicked a passerby and injured him. Could the injured man recover damages from the horse's owner? The owner argued that, unless the horse had a history of violent behavior, he should not be held liable. Holmes, writing for the court on appeal, disagreed. Holmes upheld the jury's finding that the owner was negligent in leaving what he called a "nervous" horse tethered near a sidewalk.

Holmes had once hoped that *The Common Law* would make him famous, but the book was known and read only by his fellow lawyers. Instead, he found a different satisfaction in his role as an influential state judge. Younger lawyers studied his decisions. They invited him to speak publicly. As he got used to his work, he was again able to make time for socializing. He and Fanny spent time with young writers and musicians, as well as with their older friends. Tragedy soon came to the extended Holmes family, though. Holmes's brother, Ned, died in 1884. His mother died in February 1888, followed by his sister, Amelia, in April of that year. In 1889, when Holmes's father became sick, the younger Holmes and Fanny moved back into his childhood home to care for the aging, widowed doctor. Five years later, Dr. Holmes died. Only months later, Fanny suffered a bout of rheumatic fever, which confined her to her room for months and left her permanently weakened.

One of the things that lifted Holmes's spirits was the occasional case that raised questions of broad importance. These were usually cases that required the judges to interpret the meaning of the state constitution. Such cases gave Holmes a chance to experiment with the broad legal theories that he had developed and written about before he became a judge. For example, Holmes had argued that judges should not read words in the state constitution in a way that prohibited the legislature from enacting laws that benefited society at large. He was able to make this point in the 1891 case *Commonwealth v. Perry*. The state prosecuted an employer for fining his workers, who were weavers, for mistakes in their work, such as flaws in the cloth. All the other judges held that the employer could impose such fines and that the state constitution protected the employers' right to levy fines. The legislature, they argued, could not make it a crime to do so.

Holmes dissented for the first time in his career but not for the last. It was for dissents such as this that he came to be known as the Great Dissenter. In his *Perry* dissent, Holmes stated that the constitutional guarantee protecting property was not threatened by a law prohibiting employers from fining their workers. In other words, the employer's constitutional right to property did not extend to being able to impose fines on workers. Within forty years, most American judges came to agree with his view. Dissenting opinions such as this one are important in the law's development because they often point the way to future changes in the law.

Around 1890, the Supreme Judicial Court had begun to hear cases involving labor unions. Unions are organizations of workers who want to improve their pay and working conditions by joining together to bargain with employers. Employers fear that union members will refuse to work unless their demands are met. Such

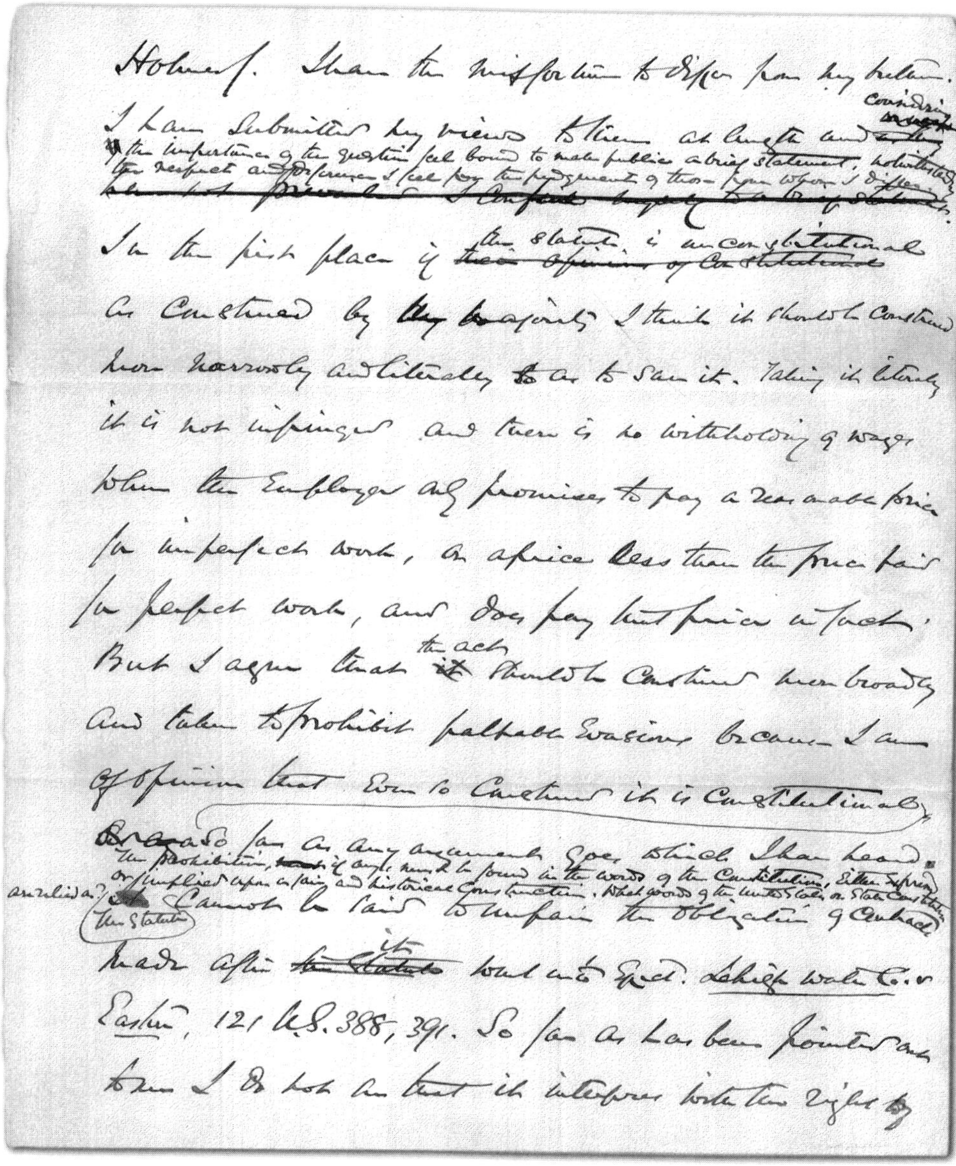

Holmes J. I have the misfortune to differ from my brethren.
I have submitted my views to them at length and considering the importance of the question feel bound to make public a brief statement, notwithstanding the respect and deference I feel for the judgment of those from whom I differ.

In the first place if the statute is unconstitutional as construed by the majority I think it should be construed more narrowly and literally so as to save it. Taking it literally it is not infringed and there is no withholding of wages when the employer only promises to pay a reasonable price for imperfect work, or a price less than the price paid for perfect work, and does pay that price in fact. But I agree that the act should be construed more broadly and taken to prohibit palpable evasions because I am of opinion that even so construed it is constitutional.

So far as any argument goes which I have heard the prohibition, if any, must be found in the words of the Constitution, either expressed or implied upon a fair and historical construction. What words of the United States or State Constitution are relied on? The statute cannot be said to impair the obligation of contracts made after it went into effect. Lehigh Water Co. v. Easton, 121 U.S. 388, 391. So far as has been pointed out to me I do not see that it interferes with the right of

Holmes's dissenting opinion in *Commonwealth v. Perry* states that the power to create reasonable laws must also prohibit "the making of unreasonable ones, and that [the contested] law is unreasonable."

refusals are known as strikes, and they sometimes end in violence. In the early 1890s, many employers tried to prevent strikes and to destroy unions by suing them, claiming that the unions interfered with business. Unlike other judges on the court, Holmes believed that workers had the right to join unions, to picket, and to strike. Holmes's view was not popular with business-men, other judges, or many leading politicians in the state, but he was willing to stand alone.

In 1896, in the case of *Vegelahn v. Guntner*, the Supreme Judicial Court forbade striking upholstery workers from picketing their employer, a furniture maker named Frederick Vegelahn, and from urging others not to work for him. Five of the seven justices who heard the case thought that both employer and possible future employees had a "liberty of contract." By this the justices meant that workers should be free to work on any terms they choose, and employers should have the same freedom to hire them on terms they find agreeable. The judges insisted that strikers interfered with this liberty. Again Holmes dissented. The issue, he argued, was the right to compete. Were the strikers' efforts to disturb Vegelahn's business justified? If a rival furniture maker were legally protected in compet-ing with Vegelahn, why should workers and unions be treated any differently? Workers, like owners of other businesses, were in competition with an employer. If the law protected business owners, it should protect

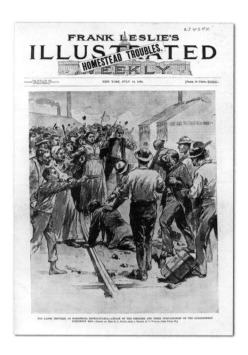

This July 1892 cover of *Frank Leslie's Illustrated Weekly* depicts the strikes at Andrew Carnegie's steel plant in Homestead, Pennsylvania. In the 1890s, tensions rose between laborers and employers as each tried to assert their rights. These disagreements sometimes ended up in court, such as in the cases of *Vegelahn v. Guntner* and *Commonwealth v. Perry*.

workers as well. Such thinking led many people to believe that Holmes was a radical who supported unions and striking workers. He was not. He merely believed that judges should not read the law in such a way as to prevent the legislature from enacting what they believed to be good public policy. He thought that the Constitution was open enough to permit democracy to flourish in this way.

In 1899, the Massachusetts court's chief justice died unexpectedly, and Holmes was appointed its new chief justice at the age of fifty-eight. He accepted the duty that went with his new title, continuing to take on a large share of the work. Despite this honor, though, Holmes continued to think of himself as someone whom no one else noticed or appreciated. He was not always confident that people valued his work. That was about to change, however, thanks to one of those unpredictable events in history, the assassination of a president.

5. An Appointment to the United States Supreme Court

In 1901, Justice Horace Gray of the U.S. Supreme Court was preparing to retire. President William McKinley and other political leaders were thinking about who might replace him. The nine justices of the U.S. Supreme Court are appointed, as are all other federal judges. When a sitting justice retires or dies, the president of the United States nominates someone to fill the vacant seat. The Constitution requires that the U.S. Senate then approve the nomination. The Senate sends the name of the nominee to its Judiciary Committee, which must first approve the selection before sending it back to the entire Senate for confirmation. Though some of Oliver Wendell Holmes Jr.'s friends put forward his name, there were other, more likely candidates. McKinley had just begun to consider candidates for the nomination when he was assassinated on September 6, 1901, by a man named Leon Czolgosz.

The next week, Vice President Theodore Roosevelt was sworn in as president, changing the politics of the Supreme Court nomination and Oliver Wendell Holmes

This silk handkerchief was created in 1901, after the assassination of the United States' 25th president, William McKinley. The handkerchief also depicts the two presidents who were assassinated before McKinley. Abraham Lincoln *(right)*, the 16th president, was assassinated in 1865. James A. Garfield *(left)*, the 20th president, was assassinated in 1881.

Jr.'s future. President Roosevelt turned to a friend, Senator Henry Cabot Lodge of Massachusetts, for advice on selecting the next justice, and Lodge recommended Holmes. It happened that Roosevelt, Lodge, and Holmes, had all gone to Harvard College, and all three had belonged to the same undergraduate social

Theodore Roosevelt (1858–1919) became the twenty-sixth president of the United States in 1901, after the assassination of William McKinley. Following Holmes's appointment to the Supreme Court, Holmes and Roosevelt became friends.

club there. These connections certainly helped Holmes's candidacy, but the new president wanted reassurances that Holmes was a reliable "party man," someone who could be trusted to support the Republican Party's political program. Roosevelt insisted to Lodge that Holmes had to be "in entire sympathy with our views." Roosevelt wanted to be sure that anyone he nominated to the Supreme Court was "absolutely sane and sound on the great national policies for which we stand."

Lodge reassured the president that Holmes's views were "sane and sound," and he arranged a meeting between Roosevelt and Holmes at the president's summer home on Long Island, New York. Roosevelt was impressed with Holmes. Lodge later told Roosevelt that the nominee was "our kind right through." The president offered Holmes what is known as a "recess appointment," meaning that the president appointed Holmes while the Senate was on recess, or vacation. Holmes continued to sit as the chief justice of the Massachusetts court until his formal confirmation by the U.S. Senate, which would take place in December 1902.

In the meantime, Massachusetts's other senator, George Frisbie Hoar, who opposed Holmes's nomination because he did not consider him suitable for the Supreme Court, began a campaign against him. "He is lacking in intellectual strength," Hoar wrote to Melville

W. Fuller, the chief justice of the U.S. Supreme Court. In light of Holmes's great accomplishments up to that time and his future success on the Supreme Court, Hoar's comment ranks as one of the most unfounded public remarks ever made about a Supreme Court justice. In the end, Hoar's campaign against Holmes had no effect, and Holmes took his seat on the bench. However, Holmes was hurt by the criticism that Hoar's opposition called forth. It left him, he told one friend, "very blue." Holmes may have appeared outwardly confident about his influence, but, like anyone else, he could be hurt by unfair criticism.

Once Holmes took his seat on the Court in December, his spirits improved. The Supreme Court, he wrote with excitement, hears "a mighty panorama of cases from every part of our great empire." It was "a center of great forces." The move to Washington, D.C., brought considerable change in the lifestyle of the Holmeses. They moved from their beloved Boston and bought a house in the nation's capital that stood about 2 miles (3.2 km) from the U.S. Capitol, where the Supreme Court sat at that time. Holmes was able to walk to and from work every day. It took him twenty-five minutes each way and provided the only physical exercise he got.

Holmes had few friends in the city. Though he liked the other justices, none became his close friends until Louis D. Brandeis was appointed to the Court in 1916.

This townhouse on Eye Street was the Holmeses' home in Washington, D.C., from 1903 to 1935. In Washington, the Holmeses' social lives became more active as they entertained and attended parties related to Holmes's appointment to the Supreme Court.

Holmes and Brandeis often agreed in their dissents. Holmes was also fond of Justice Edward Douglass White, a veteran of Louisiana's Confederate forces. Though they had fought on opposite sides in the Civil War, Holmes and White became good friends and worked together for many years. Holmes did enjoy the varied social life of the nation's capital. Throughout the year, senators and foreign ambassadors threw dinner parties. Holmes enjoyed going to

Edward Douglass White (1845–1921) was appointed associate justice of the Supreme Court in 1894. In 1910, he became the first associate justice to be appointed chief justice.

them and was especially pleased to attend White House dinners given by the man who had brought him to Washington, President Roosevelt. Shy Fanny Holmes, on the other hand, did not enjoy this kind of social life. She preferred to stay home and work on household or crafts projects. In the summer, the couple escaped Washington's heat by going to their summer home near the ocean in Beverly Farms, Massachusetts.

Holmes did not disappoint Roosevelt on most political questions. On one major issue, however, the two men

WHITE HOUSE,
WASHINGTON.

February 25, 1903.

My dear Mrs. Holmes:

Have you any engagement on Saturday evening which you wish to keep? If so pay no heed to this note, but if you have an engagement you would not mind breaking, or have no engagement, then will you and the Justice dine with me? I will have the Seth Bullocks and Moody and the William Allen Whites. Let me know in return by the bearer.

Sincerely yours,

Theodore Roosevelt

Mrs. Oliver W. Holmes,
10 Lafayette Square.

Holmes enjoyed many social opportunities in Washington, D.C. In this invitation, the Holmeses were invited to the White House to a dinner party hosted by President Theodore Roosevelt. Other guests included secretary of the navy William Henry Moody, former Deadwood, Montana, sheriff Seth Bullock, and journalist William Allen White.

did not agree. It could have brought an end to the dinner party invitations to the White House for the Holmeses. The issue involved what were known at the time as trusts. Trusts were business arrangements that often took the form of holding companies, in which one company held, or owned, all the shares of several other companies. The people who owned the holding company controlled the companies whose shares it owned. In this way, a great deal of economic and political power was concentrated in the hands of a small group of wealthy business leaders. These bankers and company presidents used holding companies and other forms of trusts to control entire industries, such as sugar and oil. These trusts bought out and destroyed their competition. Then they could raise the prices of the goods or the services they provided.

The passage of the Sherman Anti-trust Act of 1890 made illegal "every contract, combination in the form of trust or otherwise, or conspiracy, in restraint of trade among the several States." President Roosevelt was eager to create a reputation for himself as a trust-buster, someone who challenged big business leaders. Roosevelt instructed the attorney general to bring suit against the Northern Securities Company under the Anti-trust Act, hoping that the courts would find that the holding company violated antitrust policy. The Northern Securities Company held the stock of several railroads, including the Great Northern and the

A GLIMPSE INTO THE FUTURE.—FAST AND TIGHT
(President Roosevelt endeavoring to regulate the trusts by proper Government control.)
From the *Pioneer Press* (St. Paul)

Roosevelt was angered by Holmes's dissenting opinion in the Northern Securities case. Holmes, however, worked to separate legal decisions from political matters.

Northern Pacific Railroads. These companies had once competed for control of the rail routes between Minnesota and the Pacific Northwest. A federal circuit court found that the company did violate the Anti-trust Act, and, when the holding company appealed the case to the Supreme Court, five justices agreed. For a decision to pass, five of nine justices had to agree. This is known as the majority opinion. They held that the Anti-Trust Act did indeed prohibit "every contract, combination, or conspiracy" that restrained trade and business between states, and they voted to dissolve the company. President Roosevelt was pleased.

Holmes wrote a dissenting opinion in the Northern Securities case, however, in which he suggested a different reading of the Anti-Trust Act. Most important, he went on to warn his fellow justices that "Great cases like hard cases make bad law." He meant that the judges in the Northern Securities case must read the statute literally, and not allow politics to influence the case. The case was "great," or important, only because of the political controversy surrounding it. Holmes thought the judges, not the president, should decide whether the effect on interstate business was serious enough to violate the law. Holmes believed that if judges interpreted the law to reach the political result that President Roosevelt wanted, they would be making bad law corrupted by politics.

Roosevelt was annoyed that the judge he had appointed to the Supreme Court only a few years earlier should oppose his trust-busting efforts in this way. "Holmes should have been an ideal man for the bench," Roosevelt believed, but, "As a matter of fact he has been a bitter disappointment." Holmes, as would any good judge, decided cases without considering the political impact of his decisions. He sought only to understand the law, not to cater to the political interests behind a statute. Holmes remained true to that ideal throughout his career.

6. "Fundamental Principles"

Many of the cases that the U.S. Supreme Court hears present questions of constitutionality. These cases consider whether some law or act proposed by a government official violates a provision of the U.S. Constitution. In 1787, the framers of the Constitution intended to make it not only law but also the highest law. In Article VI, they provided that "This Constitution [along with federal laws and treaties]. . . shall be the supreme Law of the Land." All lawyers and judges, including the justices of the U.S. Supreme Court, must take an oath to uphold the Constitution. The president, members of Congress, and all other elected officials take the same oath, as do police officers and anyone else who wields governmental power. Bound by the Constitution as the supreme law, justices of the Supreme Court must refuse to enforce any law or government action that violates it. This responsibility is known as the power of judicial review. Each state has its own constitution, too. These constitutions are the highest law of the state, just as the U.S. Constitution is the supreme law for the entire nation.

The Constitution protects the rights of the people. To understand how it does so, and what role the U.S. Supreme Court plays, imagine a playground seesaw. Resting on one end is governmental power. This could be the power of a state legislature to control something by law, such as the price of a movie ticket. On the other side of the seesaw rests individual liberty. Individual liberty is the freedom of anyone to do whatever he or she chooses.

The Constitution of the United States was written in 1787. One of the Supreme Court's duties is to interpret the Constitution.

Suppose a state legislature, exercising its governmental power, forbids owners of movie theaters from charging more than $3 for admission to a movie. A company that owned a movie theater could claim that this law interferes with its liberty to charge whatever it wishes to people who want to see a movie there. Its freedom is on one end of the seesaw, while the government's power to limit that freedom sits on the other end. Now imagine a third person standing over the middle of the seesaw, balancing it by throwing their weight to either side to keep the forces of governmental power and individual liberty in balance. That figure represents the Supreme Court, which weighs claims of individual liberty against a state's power to regulate that liberty for the public welfare.

Consider a fictional case involving the Bill of Rights. The First Amendment, which is part of the Bill of Rights, provides in part that "Congress shall make no law respecting an establishment of religion, or prohibiting the free exercise thereof." The latter part of that sentence is called the Free Exercise Clause. Suppose a state legislature passed a law that read: "No person may attend religious services on Saturdays." The justices of the Supreme Court would hold such a law unconstitutional because it violates the Free Exercise Clause, which is part of the First Amendment and therefore the "supreme law of the land." It interferes with the free exercise of religion by those people, such as Seventh-Day Adventists or Jews, whose religions involve going to church or synagogue on Saturdays.

By the time Holmes took his seat on the bench, the Supreme Court had turned its attention to state laws that posed a similar threat to rights protected by the Constitution. The justices were especially concerned about laws that might violate what is known as the Due Process Clause of the Fourteenth Amendment. That clause provides that the government will not "deprive any person of life, liberty, or property, without due process of law." These words raise at least two

The original Bill of Rights is on display in the National Archives Building in Washington, D.C.

The Bill of Rights consists of the first ten amendments to the U.S. Constitution, which were adopted in 1791, two years after the Constitution was ratified and went into effect. They protect our most basic liberties, including freedom of speech and press; freedom from torture in criminal punishments; protections for people who are accused of a crime, such as the right to be represented by a lawyer at trial and to confront witnesses who testify against people; and the security of "life, liberty, or property," which is outlined in the Fifth Amendment.

This caricature of Holmes appeared in the August 29, 1909, *Boston Sunday Post*.

questions. What are "property" and "liberty"? What is the "due process of law"?

Holmes wrote a noted dissenting opinion involving these questions in the 1905 case of *Lochner v. New York*. The New York state legislature enacted a statute that prohibited bakers from working more than ten hours per day or sixty hours per week. The lawmakers were concerned about two public health issues. First, bakers often became sick from inhaling flour dust all day, an illness that bakery workers call white lung. Second, bakers who became sick by working long hours could contaminate baked goods and pass diseases on to the people who ate the bread they baked. In addition, long working hours also deprived bakers of time to rest or to be with their families.

Joseph Lochner was the owner of a bakery in Utica, New York, who required one of his employees to work more than ten hours per day. For this Lochner was fined for violating the statute, and the state's highest court upheld his conviction. He appealed this decision to the U.S. Supreme Court, claiming that the New York law deprived him of his liberty and his property without due process of law, in violation of the Fourteenth Amendment. Lochner's lawyers argued that the statute unconstitutionally limited an employer's right to negotiate with workers about the hours they would work. They also claimed that the law interfered with the workers' right to labor long hours.

Five of the nine Supreme Court justices agreed with Lochner and held the statute unconstitutional, while four dissented. Justice Rufus Peckham, writing for the majority, condemned the law as "mere meddlesome interferences with the rights of the individual." He warned that if New York could set maximum hours for adult men working in a bakery, there might be no limit to its powers. "We do not believe in the soundness of the views which uphold this law," he wrote indignantly. Peckham defended Lochner's "liberty of contract," which he interpreted to mean

Justice Rufus Peckham's (1838–1909) opinion in the *Lochner* case drew one of Holmes's most stinging dissents. In it, Holmes states that it is not the duty of a judge to determine the soundness of a law, but whether or not that law is constitutional.

S. .tric. .ol
Washington, IL

the power of employers to bargain with their workers about wages and hours. He declared that this power on the part of both bosses and workers was one of the liberties protected by the Due Process Clause of the Fourteenth Amendment.

Most lawyers today criticize Peckham's opinion. They think that he decided the *Lochner* case as he did because he did not like the law involved, and that he used weak constitutional arguments to justify his opinion. In the American system of government, judges are not responsible for deciding whether a law is wise. That is the job of legislatures, which appoint investigating committees, hold hearings, and call expert witnesses on the subject.

Justice Peckham's opinion provoked Holmes to write his best-known dissent, in which he argued that judges should not try to decide whether a law is good public policy or not. "I strongly believe that my agreement or disagreement [with the law] has nothing to do with the right of a majority to embody their opinions in law," he wrote. Whereas Peckham considered the case on the basis of whether the law was, in his words, "sound" or not, Holmes would strike down a law only when "a rational and fair man necessarily would admit that the statute proposed would infringe fundamental principles as they have been understood by the traditions of our people and our law."

Judges who, like Peckham, rely on due process arguments take on the job of legislators. They allow their ideas of what is wise policy to affect their interpretation of the law. They do this under the guise of making constitutional decisions. This violates the constitutional idea known as the separation of powers. That was the larger issue at stake in the debate between Justices Peckham and Holmes. In the short run, Peckham won. The New York law was struck down and could not be enforced. In the long run, however, Holmes's idea prevailed. Judges should not make judgments on laws that the Constitution entrusts to the legislatures.

7. Congress and Child Labor

Oliver Wendell Holmes Jr. and Fanny Holmes enjoyed the spring of 1918 as they did every year in Washington, D.C., frequently driving to the Potomac River to admire the beautiful cherry blossoms. When summer came that year, however, Fanny again became ill and entered the hospital for several months. Though he was worried about his wife, Holmes still worked as hard as ever. One issue was especially troubling to Americans and came before the U.S. Supreme Court that year. That issue was child labor. Child labor posed a complicated constitutional problem to lawmakers and judges, a problem rooted in the nation's system of federalism.

The U.S. government is a federal system. The federal government regulates the entire nation, and separate governments control each of the states. According to the Fourteenth Amendment, "All persons born or naturalized in the United States . . . are citizens of the United States and of the State wherein they reside." This means that U.S. citizens are citizens of both the United States and the state in which they live. The

Every spring, cherry blossoms bloom in Potomac Park in Washington, D.C. The first trees were planted in 1912 as gifts from Japan. The flowering trees, called *sakura* in Japanese, symbolize the quick passing of life because the blooms last only for a short time.

American federal system is one of the largest and most complex in the world. Only a few other nations are federal. Most nations, including France, Japan, and Zimbabwe, have only a single national government.

Such a complicated system raises questions when the laws of the states are different from the laws of the nation. The states have the power to enact laws regulating certain freedoms, and the federal government regulates others. How does the Supreme Court determine which freedoms or issues will be handled by the state government and which will be the responsibility of the federal government? What if they have competing claims? For example, states have the power to enact laws to regulate things such as the price of a movie ticket. Does Congress, the nation's legislature, have the power to regulate the price of movie tickets, too? If it did, and its law was different from a state's law, which law would override the other? The Supremacy Clause of the U.S. Constitution answers this question. It provides that "This Constitution, and the Laws of the United States . . . shall be the supreme Law of the Land. . . ." Most people interpreted the Supremacy Clause to mean that federal laws would override state laws when they conflicted. Holmes and his fellow justices, however, did not always agree with that interpretation.

The Constitution's two most important provisions relating to federalism are the Commerce Clause and the Tenth Amendment. The Commerce Clause reads, "The Congress shall have power . . . to regulate Commerce . . . among the several States. . . ." The Tenth Amendment states that "the powers not delegated to the United States by the Constitution, nor prohibited by it to the States, are reserved to the States respectively, or to the people." Neither of these clauses provides clear guidance for deciding day-to-day issues. What happens if Congress's regulation conflicts with that of a state? The justices of the Supreme Court nevertheless looked to these clauses hopefully. They sought clues about what the framers of the Constitution might have thought about modern problems.

Such constitutional problems of federalism became most troubling in two cases that together are known as the child labor cases, decided in 1918 and 1922. At that time, boys and girls as young as eight or nine years old worked ten-hour days, six and sometimes seven days per week, in coal mines, cotton mills, factories, and on farms. State governments did not require children to go to school for nine months of the year, as they do now. Some states did not require school attendance at all. Poor parents might hope to send their children to school, knowing that education was the surest road out of poverty, but they often had no choice but to send them to work instead. The pay that children brought home, little though it always was, was sometimes all that kept their families from starvation. Working long hours weakened the children's health, and the machinery that they tended often injured them. They were thrown into the dangerous, brutal world of factory labor. Children accepted lower wages than adults did, and children were not likely to join unions. They would not demand higher pay or shorter hours. One of the people involved in a child labor case in 1918 weighed only 105 pounds (47.6 kg) at the age of twenty. He had this to say about his experience as a child worker: "The years I've put in

These two boys are mending threads on a spinning frame at a textile factory called Bibb Mill in Macon, Georgia. The photographer, Lewis Wickes Hine, was hired in 1908 by the National Child Labor Committee to document child labor in the United States.

a cotton mill have stunted my growth. They kept me from getting any schooling. I had to stop school after the third grade and now I need the education I didn't get. . . . From 12 years on, I was working 12 hours a day—from 6 in the morning till 7 at night, with time out for meals. And sometimes I worked nights besides." Nearly everyone, the public and lawmakers alike, thought that child labor was wrong. As Holmes himself wrote, "If there is any matter upon which civilized countries have agreed . . . it is the evil of premature and excessive child labor."

In 1916, Congress decided to tackle the problem. The Constitution does not empower Congress to prohibit child labor outright. The legislation had to be rooted in the principles of the Constitution. Congress addressed the issue as a question of interstate trade and passed legislation under the authority of the Commerce Clause. The Keating-Owen Child Labor Act prohibited trade goods, such as coal or furniture, processed by child workers from being shipped across state lines. Most products move in what is called interstate commerce, or from one state to another. If a federal law made it impossible for products made by child labor to be shipped from one state to another, businesses that wished to maintain a profitable trade would be compelled to stop using child laborers.

Many industries, especially cotton mills and furniture factories, resisted this law because they profited by using children as workers. These companies began a suit

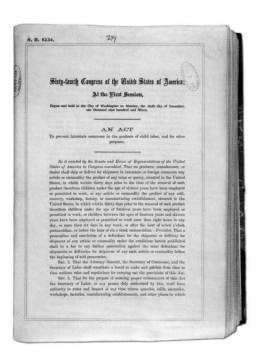

The Keating-Owen Child Labor Act of 1916 was ruled unconstitutional by the Supreme Court, which said that the government had no right to regulate interstate commerce.

seeking to have the Child Labor Act overturned. This case, known as *Hammer v. Dagenhart*, was decided in 1918. A majority of five of the nine justices of the U.S. Supreme Court found the Child Labor Act unconstitutional. The Supreme Court held that Congress did not have the power to forbid interstate shipping of products that were harmless in themselves. There is nothing inherently dangerous in a lump of coal or a table. These five justices thought that Congress could forbid only dangerous things, such as explosives or diseased cattle, from crossing state lines. The act was meant to control the production of goods, specifically goods made by children. It would not control the shipping or the sale of these goods. As such, the statute violated the Tenth Amendment. Per the 1918 decision, the issue of child labor was not directly mentioned in the Constitution, so its regulation fell under the authority of the state governments.

Holmes disagreed and was joined only by his friend

Justice Louis D. Brandeis. In his dissenting opinion, Holmes insisted that Congress had the power to regulate interstate trade and the power to stop interstate shipment of things made by children. He warned that judges cannot decide a case based on whether a law was wise or not, which is what he thought the majority of the court was doing in this case. He felt that the other justices were making their decision based on their feelings against child labor, rather than on the matter of interstate trade. The Supreme Court has to decide cases based on whether or not they conflict with the Constitution. "This Court [should not] intrude its judgment upon questions of policy or morals," he wrote.

Congress was shocked by the Court's decision, as was the American public. Child labor was a serious problem, and many Americans believed it was Congress's job to protect the citizens. In 1922, legislators returned to the problem. In a second statute, Congress tried to end child labor by laying a special tax on products produced in factories where children worked. They reasoned that if a table produced in a factory where children worked were to cost more than one produced only by adult labor because of the tax, no one would buy the more expensive table, and companies would stop hiring children.

The Supreme Court once again disappointed the American people by holding that second statute unconstitutional as well, in a case titled *Bailey v. Drexel*

Furniture Company. The Supreme Court claimed that Congress was not simply enacting a tax, but rather was attempting to regulate child labor indirectly. As the Court had already decided, this was not the job of the federal government. The justices in their majority opinion insisted that Congress could not use its taxing power to regulate matters under the authority of the state government. Americans were shocked and disgusted by the Court's opinion. Many states endorsed an amendment to the Constitution that would plainly and openly give Congress power to prohibit child labor, but the states never ratified this amendment. Instead the states gradually took care of the problem by enacting stricter school attendance laws, and by simply prohibiting the use of child labor. In later cases, the Court reversed its decision on the *Hammer* and *Bailey* cases and overruled them. Thus Oliver Wendell Holmes's ideas about interpreting the law without making a judgment about policy prevailed.

8. Free Speech and the First Amendment

Can the government punish somebody for speaking or writing something, especially an opinion about a political topic? The U.S. Constitution protects all speech that does not encourage someone to commit a criminal act. The government can prohibit a person from urging someone to kill another person and can punish him or her for doing so. Where does the government draw the line between speech that challenges the law and speech that encourages people to break the law? How do the courts determine whether an act of speech falls into the latter category? The First Amendment to the Constitution provides a general guideline. It says, "Congress shall make no law . . . abridging the freedom of speech, or of the press." Yet what is "freedom of speech" as protected by the First Amendment?

Before Justice Oliver Wendell Holmes Jr.'s 1902 appointment, the Supreme Court had decided very few cases involving issues of the First Amendment. In American law, when a court decides a case, a precedent is set. Every case thereafter that is based on the same legal principle should be decided in a way that follows the precedent-setting case. The precedent is binding on later courts, which must follow its rule of law. In the case of the First Amendment, the Court did not have many precedents by 1918 to guide their decision. In the first years of the twentieth century, most Americans assumed that governments had broad powers to suppress any act of speech that most people deemed offensive. Holmes believed that certain kinds of speech were not protected by the First Amendment. Three of his early decisions illustrate his understanding of the law.

The first was *McAuliffe v. Mayor and Board of Aldermen of New Bedford*, which was decided by the Supreme Judicial Court of Massachusetts in 1892. McAuliffe was a police officer who had raised money for a political candidate. It was against the police regulation to collect money for political purposes or to join political committees. In response, the mayor promptly fired him, and the police officer sued to get his job back. Holmes, speaking for the Massachusetts court, upheld the power of the city government to fire McAuliffe. A police officer "may have a constitutional right to talk politics," Holmes wrote in his majority opinion, "but he has no constitutional right to be a policeman." Holmes explained that the city could require some of its employees, such as police officers and firefighters, to give up some of their First Amendment rights as a condition for holding their jobs. If a city employee violated this policy, he had no special right to keep his job.

In the 1895 case of *Commonwealth v. Davis*, a lay minister was fined for preaching sermons on Sunday mornings in Boston Common, a large public park in the middle of the city, without a special permit to do so. Holmes saw nothing wrong with requiring such a permit. He thought that because the Boston city government had the right to close the Common completely, it had the authority to control what people did there, including the expression of political or religious opinions. He saw this power as being no different from

The U.S. Supreme Court justices in 1903 were *(back row, from left)* Oliver Wendell Holmes Jr., Rufus Peckham, Joseph McKenna, William Rufus Day, *(front row, from left)* Henry Billings Brown, John Marshall Harlan, Melville Weston Fuller, David Josiah Brewer, Edward Douglass White.

This photograph of Boston Common was taken in 1895, around the time of the *Commonwealth v. Davis* case. Holmes argued that the case was not one of free speech, but rather "directed toward the modes in which Boston Common may be used."

homeowners' rights to keep unwanted strangers out of their homes.

As a member of the U.S. Supreme Court, Holmes used similar logic to decide the appeal in *Patterson v. Colorado* (1907). A newspaper editor had written an editorial that criticized the way in which the state supreme court was handling a case. The editorial was considered a form of speech, and the court found the editor in contempt of court and fined him. Holmes upheld the power of the judge to do so. His justification was the "prior restraint" test. Under this rule of law, the state could not prohibit people from saying or writing anything before they did so, but it could freely punish them afterward. It did not matter whether the speech was true or not, either. "The preliminary freedom extends as well to the false as to the true; the subsequent punishment may extend as well to the true as to the false," Holmes wrote.

By 1910, Holmes had developed a strong position on the meaning of free speech and the First Amendment. Cases decided by the U.S. Supreme Court before World War I did not offer much protection for people who spoke out politically. Holmes's decisions, in their literal reading of the law, helped to give the state a great deal of power to suppress speech and writing that most people found offensive. People even went to prison for criticizing government officials. When America entered World War I, however, all that would begin to change, and Holmes would be largely responsible for those changes as well.

9. World War I Changes Everything

In June 1914, Serbian nationalists assassinated the heir to the Austro-Hungarian throne, Archduke Francis Ferdinand, and his wife, Sophie, while they were on a state visit to Sarajevo, which was then a part of Serbia. In response, the Austro-Hungarian Empire declared war on Serbia, with its ally, Germany, following suit. Russia entered the war to defend Serbia, and France joined Russia in order to attack its enemy, Germany. Germany attacked Belgium, which drew Great Britain into the conflict because of its alliance with Belgium. Thus World War I began. At first, civilians on both sides believed they would enjoy a quick, easy victory, but the war dragged on, and the death toll mounted. On the western front, Germany and Austria-Hungary, known as the Central Powers, battled Great Britain and France, known as the Allies. Many soldiers died on both sides, but neither was able to defeat the other. On the eastern front, German armies defeated Russian forces in Poland, killing thousands of soldiers and taking tens of thousands of prisoners.

The June 29, 1914, edition of *Le Petit Parisien* announces the assassination of Archduke Francis Ferdinand and his wife, Sophie. Gavrilo Princip, a Serb nationalist, killed the couple. Princip wished to destroy the Austro-Hungarian state and to create a Slavic nation from the Balkan states, which included Serbia, Croatia, and Slovenia.

Watching these events with shock and disbelief, Americans were determined to stay out of the war. They hoped to follow a policy of neutrality and to engage the two sides in an organized plan for peace, but they did not succeed. The war dragged on for three long years, during which time America signaled its support of the Allies by sending far more supplies to Great Britain and France than it did to their enemies, Germany and Austria-Hungary. In retaliation, German U-boats, or submarines, sank American passenger ships. In response the United States declared war and joined the Allies in 1917. The American declaration of war was a turning point in the conflict. Germany would soon show signs of weakness, and the war would end in November 1918. However, the Bolshevik Revolution and the rise of a Communist government in the new Soviet Union under Vladimir Lenin in November 1917 would change the nature of the war. During the next month, Lenin ordered Russian troops to lay down their arms, and he signed a peace treaty with the Central Powers.

To withdraw from the war, Lenin (1870–1924) was forced to give Russian territory in Poland, Ukraine, and Caucasia to the Central Powers. In March 1918, the Bolshevik government signed the Brest-Litovsk peace agreement, ending the war with Germany.

A small but vocal group of Americans, many of German American heritage, did not think the United States should have entered the war. Some American Socialists thought the Allied invasion of the Soviet Union in 1917, staged to revive an eastern front against the Germans, was an effort to destroy the new Communist government there. Some criticized the government openly, and the government prosecuted them for violation of the Espionage and Sedition Acts of 1917 and 1918. These laws made criticizing government officials and policies a federal crime. They made it illegal to interfere with the government's recruitment of soldiers and sailors, to spread false information about the war, to spy for an enemy, to criticize the government, the army, or the flag, and to interrupt the production of materials necessary to the war effort. Congress was trying to stifle any criticism of the American policies in World War I.

The first of these cases to be appealed to the Supreme Court was *Schenck v. United States*, which came before the Court in 1918. Charles Schenck was a German American and a member of the Socialist Party who had criticized America's war policy and distributed leaflets that urged young men not to join the armed forces. He was convicted under the Espionage Act on the grounds that his words might persuade American men not to enlist in the U.S. Army or Navy. Holmes, speaking for a unanimous Court, upheld Schenck's conviction.

In his written opinion, Holmes provided some basic

tests to determine whether the First Amendment protects political speech like Schenck's. The amendment does not "protect a man in falsely shouting fire in a theater," he wrote. He determined that Schenck's criticisms were groundless. The question, he continued, is whether the speech will "create a clear and present danger" and whether it will cause "evils that Congress has a right to prevent." Holmes determined that Schenck's intent was to encourage a "bad tendency," a behavior considered offensive by most people, and, in this case, one that posed a threat to American security. The clear-and-present-danger test remains a key to understanding the First Amendment today.

Other judges, however, studied Holmes's reasoning and interpreted his words to mean that all critics of the government should be considered for punishment. This worried Holmes. "The federal judges seem to me to have got hysterical about the war," he wrote to a friend. Holmes began to rethink his ideas about the First Amendment, and he applied these new ideas in the 1919 appeal of *Abrams v. United States*. Five teenage Russian Jewish immigrants had been convicted for publishing leaflets that opposed the American presence in the Soviet Union and urged local factory workers to go on strike, arguing that they were making the weapons that would be used to fight the Russians. The five argued that their right to free speech had been violated. The Court upheld the convictions and long prison sentences of the defendants, but Holmes dissented. He thought it was wrong to send five teenagers to prison for twenty years or more just because they had urged changes in government policy. He thought that the other justices applied his clear-and-present-danger test inappropriately. He insisted that "the principle of the right to free speech is always the same" in both war and peacetime. "I believe the defendants had as much right to publish [their leaflets] as the government has to publish the Constitution," he insisted.

Holmes had changed his views about free speech. In a long passage at the end of his opinion, he set forth his beliefs about the place of the First Amendment in American society. He had come to believe in what he called the "free trade in ideas." He wrote that "the best test of truth is the power of the thought to get itself accepted in the competition of the market." This has come to be known as the "marketplace of ideas" approach, and it remains a basis for interpreting the First Amendment today. At that time, however, most Americans did not agree with Holmes, and he felt discouraged. "I fear we have less freedom of speech here than they have in England," he wrote to an English friend.

With the end of World War I in November 1918, the states began to prosecute Americans who had joined the Communist Party, which had gained a following after the war. In the 1925 case *Gitlow v. New York*, the Supreme Court upheld New York's conviction of a man

In this undated photograph, Holmes *(left)* and Brandeis (1856–1941) are walking down the street. The two justices often shared minority opinions in the Court. Brandeis University, which opened in 1948 in Waltham, Massachusetts, is named in Brandeis's honor.

who had founded the Communist Party in that state. Holmes, along with his friend Justice Louis D. Brandeis, dissented. Holmes pointed out that the Communist Party and those who created it had no present intent to "overthrow the state by force and violence." He continued, "If in the long run the beliefs" held by the Communist Party are to gain acceptance, "the only meaning of free speech is that they should be given their chance and have their way." Holmes did not agree with Communist theories, but he believed that the First Amendment protects all people, even those with ideas that most other Americans consider extreme. The Constitution, as he had written in his opinion for the *Lochner* case, "is made for people of fundamentally differing views."

When Justice Holmes retired from the Court in 1932, his ideas about the First Amendment had not yet become accepted by either the federal judicial system or the public at large. Holmes did not live to see that day. Gradually Holmes's dissenting arguments persuaded lawyers and judges, including the justices of the Supreme Court. Eventually Court decisions confirmed Holmes's and Brandeis's dissenting opinions regarding the interpretation of the First Amendment. Legal scholars began to look to Holmes's opinions as well. The modern Court agrees that the danger to society posed by an act of speech must indeed be truly serious and immediate before the state can prohibit it.

10. Final Years

In December 1900, when he was almost sixty years old, Oliver Wendell Holmes Jr. paused to consider aging. "Life seems short," he wrote to his friend Henry James, "one's remaining friends few & solitude near—but I shall catch some new ones if necessary & generally I feel about as keen as I did at 20 & have a damned sight better time." Holmes did not know then that he would live more than thirty years longer.

Once tall and proud in his bearing, Holmes became stooped as he grew older. His life outside the Court grew more quiet. He relied on his secretaries to help him with simple tasks, such as getting up from his reading chair or putting on his shoes. He took a walk each afternoon, accompanied by a secretary. He had spent many hours standing at the desk that had once belonged to his grandfather, writing letters to his many friends. Fanny continued to read to him in the

---

Opposite: This portrait of Holmes was painted in 1931 by Charles Sidney Hopkinson. It is on display in the lower Great Hall of the Supreme Court in Washington, D.C.

evening. Friends and visitors came to spend time with him at home, and Holmes still enjoyed the company of younger people. He kept his sense of humor, even about the troubles of old age. "Kindly remain alive," Holmes told a close friend. "Even my haircutter has died."

Holmes kept up an admirable pace at work. His one last ambition was to write an opinion for the Court at the age of ninety. In March 1928, at the age of 87, he became the oldest man ever to sit as a justice on the Supreme Court, and it seemed that he would likely reach his goal.

Less than a year later, however, Fanny slipped and fell in the bathtub, breaking her hip. Bedridden for three months, she grew weaker and finally died. To a close friend Holmes wrote, "For sixty years she made life poetry for me." With Fanny gone, Holmes lost much of his enthusiasm for life. "I shall keep at work and interested while it lasts—though not caring very much for how long," he wrote to a friend. "I like to live," he wrote to another friend, "but feel that it does not matter much." To still another, he wrote that "life has been so much better than I ever dreamed it could be . . . and yet I don't know whether I should care to live it over again."

The elderly chief justice, former president William Howard Taft, had health problems of his own. He resigned from the Court early in 1930. As the senior member of the Court, Holmes became the acting chief

Holmes's friendship with English legal scholar Sir Frederick Pollock (1845–1937) lasted for more than sixty years. In this 1929 letter to Pollock, Holmes writes of the death of his wife, Fanny. A book of the correspondence between Holmes and Pollock was published in 1941.

justice. He took on the responsibility with care, presiding over the judicial conferences and summarizing cases quickly and efficiently, much to the delight of the other justices. On February 24, 1930, President Herbert Hoover nominated Charles Evans Hughes to be the new chief justice. This pleased Holmes. He knew the Court was in capable hands.

Holmes continued to receive visits from old friends, former secretaries, and other justices. As Holmes's ninetieth birthday approached, the honors began to pour in. Issues of law journals were dedicated to him, the American Bar Association gave him a gold medal, and Holmes agreed to mark the occasion in a radio address. His words were broadcast to the nation from his library. Holmes said, "The riders in a race do not stop short when they reach the goal. There is a little finishing canter before coming to a standstill. There is time to hear the kind voice of friends and to say to one's self: 'The work is done.'"

Holmes's health worsened. He had greater difficulty reading and writing, which took much of the pleasure of life from him. Holmes accepted his difficulties gracefully. In a letter to his friend Sir Frederick Pollock, he wrote, "I am being happily idle." Finally, in January 1932, Holmes resigned from the Court. The work had become a burden. In retirement, he stayed exclusively at home in Washington, D.C. His secretary continued to visit the house every day to read to Holmes and to help him with household and personal chores. Holmes continued to receive visitors, but he was not interested in news and politics. "It's all very remote to me . . ." he explained. "I'm like a ghost on the battlefield with bullets flying through me." He often thought about his greatest passion. "What a profession the law is!" he wrote in 1885. "In what other does one plunge so deep in the stream of life—so share its passions, its battles, its despair, its triumphs?" In February 1935, Holmes

This 1932 political cartoon by Carl Rose imagines how the next appointed Supreme Court justice, Benjamin Cardozo, might feel taking over Holmes's seat in the Court.

caught a cold. It quickly developed into pneumonia, and he died peacefully at home the following month, on March 6.

• • • • •

Oliver Wendell Holmes Jr. often contemplated the roles of great people and great thinkers in history. Holmes was speaking of himself when he said, in 1886, that "a man may live greatly in the law as well as elsewhere . . . there as well as elsewhere he may wreak

Oliver Wendell Holmes Jr. is buried in Arlington National Cemetery in Arlington, Virginia. Arlington, officially designated as a military ceme-tery in 1864, has the graves of veterans from every U.S. war and con-flict. Holmes's headstone describes his Civil War service as well as his years as a Justice in the U.S. Supreme Court.

himself upon life, may drink the bitter cup of heroism, may wear his heart out after the unattainable." He added, "To think great thoughts, you must be heroes as well as idealists."

In 1886, Holmes had delivered a formal address on what it means to be a lawyer. With himself in mind, he spoke of "the secret isolated joy of the thinker, who knows that, a hundred years after he is dead and forgotten, men who never heard of him will be moving to the measure of his thought." His words were an amazing prediction of his own influence. American law today marches to the measure of Oliver Wendell Holmes Jr.'s thinking. He was wrong about only one thing: He was not forgotten. The Union soldier who became a lawyer, then a state judge, and finally a justice of the U.S. Supreme Court is remembered as the man who changed American law forever.

Timeline

1841	Oliver Wendell Holmes Jr. is born in Boston on March 8.
1857	In October, Holmes enters Harvard College.
1861	In April, Holmes enlists in the Massachusetts Volunteer Infantry.
	In June, Holmes graduates from Harvard College.
	Holmes is wounded at Ball's Bluff, Virginia, on October 21.
1862	Holmes is wounded at Antietam (Sharpsburg), Maryland, on September 17.
1863	Holmes is wounded at Chancellorsville, Virginia, on May 3.
1864	In July, Holmes resigns his commission.
	In October, he enters Harvard Law School.
1866	Holmes graduates from Harvard Law School in June.
1866–1882	Holmes practices law in Boston.
1872	Holmes marries Fanny Dixwell on June 17.
1872–1873	Holmes edits the *American Law Review*.
1881	Holmes publishes *The Common Law*.
1882	Holmes becomes Weld Professor of Law, Harvard Law School.
	In December, Holmes is appointed a justice of the Supreme Judicial Court of Massachusetts.
1891	Holmes dissents in *Commonwealth v. Perry*.
1896	Holmes dissents in *Vegelahn v. Guntner*.

1899–1902	Holmes serves as chief justice of the Supreme Judicial Court of Massachusetts.
1902	In December, Holmes is sworn in as a justice of the U.S Supreme Court.
1904	Holmes dissents in *Northern Securities Co. v. United States*.
1905	Holmes dissents in *Lochner v. New York*.
1917	The United States declares war on Germany in April.
1918	Holmes dissents in *Hammer v. Dagenhart*.
	Holmes writes for the Court in *Schenck v. United States*.
1919	Holmes dissents in *Abrams v. United States*.
1922	Holmes dissents in *Bailey v. Drexel Furniture Company*.
1925	Holmes dissents in *Gitlow v. New York*.
1929	Fanny Dixwell Holmes dies on April 30.
1931	Holmes gives his ninetieth birthday radio address on March 8.
1932	Holmes resigns from the U.S. Supreme Court on January 11.
1935	Oliver Wendell Holmes Jr. dies on March 6.

Glossary

abolish (uh-BAH-lish) To do away with.

abridging (uh-BRIJ-ing) Lessening or cutting short something, such as the freedom of speech.

alliance (uh-LY-unts) A close association formed between people or groups of people to reach a common objective.

amputated (AM-pyoo-tayt-ed) To have cut off or removed, especially to have removed a limb by surgery.

aristocratic (uh-ris-tuh-KRA-tik) Having the tastes, opinions, and manners of the upper class.

assassination (uh-sa-sih-NAY-shun) The killing of an important person.

bench (BENCH) A court. Courts are called benches because, centuries ago, the judges either sat on benches or wrote on them.

commission (kuh-MIH-shun) A document that gives a certain military rank or authority.

Communist (KOM-yuh-nist) Belonging to a political party that believes in a system in which all the land, houses, and factories belong to the government and are shared by everyone.

confirmation (kon-fer-MAY-shun) Approval by the U.S. Senate of someone the president nominates to a federal office.

Congress (KON-gres) The part of the U.S. government that makes laws and is made of the House of Representatives and the Senate. The members of Congress are chosen by the people of each state.

contempt (kun-TEMPT) A punishment of a fine or a jail sentence, given by a judge to people who disrupt a trial.

disputes (dis-PYOOTS) Arguments or disagreements.

dissents (dih-SENTS) Opinions written by a judge who disagrees with the result that a majority of the other judges reach.

dysentery (DIH-sun-ter-ee) A disease marked by severe diarrhea and the passage of mucus and blood.

immigrants (IH-muh-grints) People who move to a new country from another country.

journals (JER-nulz) Magazines that present information about a specific subject, such as law or medicine.

judiciary (joo-DIH-shee-er-ee) Referring to a system of courts of justice. In the United States, "judiciary" refers to the whole body of judges, both state and federal.

jurisprudence (juhr-is-PROO-dents) The system or body of law and the study of this system in law school.

Justice (JUS-tis) Another word for a judge, particularly one who sits on the Supreme Court.

lay minister (LAY MIH-nih-ster) An unofficial minister who is not a member of the clergy.

leaflets (LEEF-lets) Printed, folded paper handbills used to try to convince others of an opinion.

majority (muh-JOR-ih-tee) More than half. In the Supreme Court, five or more of the nine judges make up a majority.

maritime (MAR-ih-tym) Having to do with the sea, ships, or sea travel.

muskets (MUS-kits) Long-barreled firearms used by soldiers before the invention of the rifle.

negligent (NEH-glih-jent) Careless of how one's actions might hurt others.

opinions (uh-PIN-yunz) Justices' written explanations for their decisions in cases. If most of the other justices agree with a justice's opinion, it is the "majority opinion." If not, it is the "dissenting opinion."

overruled (oh-ver-ROOLD) Rejected a decision. Sometimes a court decides that one of its earlier decisions was wrong. The court "overrules" it, holding that it is no longer a valid judgment about what the law is.

picket (PIH-ket) To walk or stand around in front of something as a protest.

precedent (PREH-sih-dent) A legal decision that is used as an example to decide future cases.

prosecuted (PRAH-sih-kyoot-ed) Took legal action against someone for the purpose of punishment.

pseudonym (SOO-doh-nim) A made-up name, also called a pen name, because it is often used by writers.

ratified (RA-tih-fyd) Approved or agreed to something in an official way.

seceded (sih-SEED-ed) Withdrew from a group or a country.

Socialists (SOH-shuh-lists) Members of a political party that believes in a system in which there is no private property.

solitary (SAH-lih-ter-ee) Liking to be alone.

statute (STA-choot) A law that is enacted by the legislative body of a government.

territory (TER-uh-tor-ee) Land that is controlled by a person or a group of people.

transitory (TRAN-zih-tor-ee) Brief or short-lived.

trifling (TRY-fling) Not very important; minor.

unanimous (yoo-NA-nih-mus) Having the agreement of all.

void (VOYD) Not legal; not enforceable.

western front (WES-tern FRUNT) The western border of a war, including all lands and countries that are fighting in the war along that border.

Additional Resources

To learn more about Oliver Wendell Holmes Jr. and the Supreme Court, check out these books and Web sites:

Books

Patrick, John J. *The Young Oxford Companion to the Supreme Court of the United States*. New York: Oxford University Press, 1994.

White, G. Edward. *Oliver Wendell Holmes: Sage of the Supreme Court*. New York: Oxford University Press, 2000.

Web Sites

Due to the changing nature of Internet links, PowerPlus Books has developed an online list of Web sites related to the subject of this book. This site is updated regularly. Please use this link to access the list: www.powerkidslinks.com/lalt/holmes/

Bibliography

Baker, Liva. *The Justice from Beacon Hill: The Life and Times of Oliver Wendell Holmes*. New York: HarperCollins, 1991.

Bowen, Catherine Drinker. *Yankee from Olympus: Justice Holmes and His Family*. Boston: Little, Brown, and Co., 1945.

Burton, Steven J. (ed.) *The Path of Law and Its Influence: The Legacy of Oliver Wendell Holmes, Jr*. New York: Cambridge University Press, 2000.

Howe, Mark DeWolfe. *Justice Oliver Wendell Holmes: The Proving Years*. Cambridge, MA: Harvard University Press, 1963.

Howe, Mark DeWolfe. *Justice Oliver Wendell Holmes: The Shaping Years*. Cambridge, MA: Harvard University Press, 1957.

Lerner, Max. *The Mind and Faith of Justice Holmes: His Speeches, Essays, Letters, and Judicial Opinions*. New York: Modern Library, 1954.

Monagan, John S. *The Grand Panjandrum: The Mellow Years of Justice Holmes*. Lanham, MD: University Press of America, 1988.

Novick, Sheldon M. *The Collected Works of Justice Holmes: Complete Public Writings and Selected Judicial Opinions of Oliver Wendell Holmes*. Chicago: University of Chicago Press, 1995.

Novick, Sheldon M. *Honorable Justice: The Life of Oliver Wendell Holmes*. Boston: Little, Brown, and Co., 1989.

Posner, Richard A. *The Essential Holmes: Selections from the Letters, Speeches, Judicial Opinions, and Other Writings of Oliver Wendell Holmes, Jr*. Chicago: University of Chicago Press, 1992.

White, G. Edward. *Justice Oliver Wendell Holmes: Law and the Inner Self*. New York: Oxford University Press, 1993.

Index

A

Abrams v. United States, 88
American Bar Association, 96
American Revolution, 8
Army of the Potomac, 25, 30
Article VI, 62
Autocrat of the Breakfast Table, The, 14

B

Bailey v. Drexel Furniture Company, 77–78
Ball's Bluff, Virginia, 24–25
Battle of Antietam, 26
Beacon Hill, 11, 13, 40
Beverly Farms, Massachusetts, 57
Bill of Rights, 64
Bolshevik Revolution, 86
Boston, Massachusetts, 8–9, 11–14, 16, 25–26, 30–32, 35–36, 41, 55, 81
Boston Brahmins, 13
Brandeis, Louis D., 55, 57, 76, 89, 91

C

Chancellorsville, Virginia, 30
Child Labor Act, 75–76
Civil War, 5, 20, 24, 30, 57
Commerce Clause, 72, 75
Common Law, The, 36–38, 45
Commonwealth v. Davis, 81
Commonwealth v. Perry, 46
Czolgosz, Leon, 51

D

Dixwell, Fanny, 32. *See also* Fanny Holmes
Due Process Clause, 64, 68

E

Emancipation Proclamation, 26
Espionage Act, 87

F

Ferdinand, Francis, 84
First Amendment, 64, 79–80, 83, 87–89, 91
Fort Sumter, 20
Fourteenth Amendment, 64, 67–68, 70
Fourth Battalion of Massachusetts Volunteers, 20
Free Exercise Clause, 64
Fuller, Melville W., 54–55

G

Gitlow v. New York, 89
Governor's Council, 39
Gray, Horace, 51

H

Hallowell, Norwood Penrose, 19–20
Hammer v. Dagenhart, 76, 78
Hampton, Virginia, 25
Harvard College, 5, 8–9, 17, 19–20, 52
Harvard Law School, 32, 38–39
Harvard Medical School, 9–10
Hasty Pudding Club, 19
Hoar, George Frisbie, 54–55
Holmes, Abiel (grandfather), 9
Holmes, Amelia (grandmother), 9
Holmes, Amelia (mother), 16, 45. *See also* Amelia Jackson
Holmes, Amelia (sister), 11, 45
Holmes, Edward or Ned (brother), 12, 45
Holmes, Fanny (wife), 34–35, 38, 40, 42, 45, 57, 70, 94. *See also* Fanny Dixwell
Holmes, Oliver Wendell, Sr. (father), 8–9, 13–14, 32, 39–40, 45

Hoover, Herbert, 95
Hughes, Charles Evans, 95

J
Jackson, Amelia (mother), 11. *See also* Amelia Holmes
Jackson, Charles (grandfather), 11, 42
James, Henry, 92
judicial review, 7, 62

L
Lee, Robert E., 26, 30
Lenin, Vladimir, 86
Lincoln, Abraham, 20, 26
Lochner, Joseph, 66–67
Lochner v. New York, 66, 68, 91
Lodge, Henry Cabot, 12–13, 52, 54
London, England, 13, 35
Long Island, New York, 54

M
Mattapoisett, Massachusetts, 35
McAuliffe v. Mayor and Board of Aldermen of New Bedford, 80
McKinley, William, 51

N
Northern Securities Company, 59–60

P
Paris, France, 9
Patterson v. Colorado, 82
Peckham, Rufus, 67–69
Pollock, Sir Frederick, 96
Porcellian Club, 19
Potomac River, 22, 26, 70

R
Roosevelt, Theodore, 5, 51–52, 54, 57, 59–61

S
Sarajevo, Serbia, 84
Schenck, Charles, 87–88
Schenck v. United States, 87
Sedition Act, 87
Seven Days' Battle, 26
Shattuck, George, 32, 35, 39
Sherman Anti-trust Act, 59–60
Supremacy Clause, 72
Supreme Judicial Court of Massachusetts, 5, 11, 32, 38–41, 43, 46, 48–49, 80

T
Taft, William Howard, 94
Tenth Amendment, 72, 76
Twentieth Massachusetts Volunteer Infantry Regiment, 20, 22, 24, 26–27

U
U.S. Capitol, 55
U.S. Congress, 7, 62, 72, 75–78, 88
U.S. Constitution, 7, 49, 51, 62–63, 69, 72–73, 75–76, 78–79, 89, 91
U.S. Senate, 51, 54
U.S. Supreme Court, 5, 7, 51, 54–55, 60–64, 67, 70–72, 76–79, 81–83, 87–89, 91–92, 94–96, 99

V
Vegelahn, Frederick, 48
Vegelahn v. Guntner, 48

W
Washington, D.C., 26, 55, 57, 70, 96
White, Edward Douglass, 57
White House, 57, 59
World War I, 83–84, 87, 89

About the Authors

Sophie W. Littlefield writes on subjects as diverse as technology, parenting, and quilting. She lives in Northern California with her husband and two children. She couldn't ask for a better co-author than her dad.

William M. Wiecek is a legal historian who teaches at Syracuse University College of Law. He has written or edited seven books, six of them dealing with constitutional history and the history of the United States Supreme Court. This is the first collaboration between the authors as a daughter-father writing team, and they had a lot of fun doing it together.

Primary Sources

Cover. Oliver Wendell Holmes Jr., oil on canvas, 1913, Wilton Lockwood, Courtesy of the Social Law Library, Boston. **Page 4.** Oliver Wendell Holmes Jr., photograph, 1910, Pach Brothers, Courtesy of Art & Visual Materials, Special Collections Department, Harvard Law School Library. **Page 8.** View of the Town Hall, Boston, Colored engraving, eighteenth century, Franz Xavier Habermann, Lauros/Giraudon/Bridgeman Art Library. **Page 9.** "Under Ether." Photograph, 1846, © Hulton/Archive/Getty Images. **Page 10.** *Old Ironsides*. Painting, Michele Felice Corné, Courtesy of the U.S. Naval Academy Museum. This is part of a four-panel series of the encounter between the USS Constitution and the HMS Guerrière. **Page 11.** Amelia Lee Jackson Holmes. Photograph, 1875, Courtesy of Art & Visual Materials, Special Collections Department, Harvard Law School Library. **Page 12.** The Holmes Children: Edward, Amelia, Oliver Jr. photograph, 1855, Courtesy of Art & Visual Materials, Special Collections Department, Harvard Law School Library. **Page 15.** *The Autocrat of the Breakfast Table*. 1886, Spy (Leslie Matthew Ward), Courtesy of Art & Visual Materials, Special Collections Department, Harvard Law School Library. **Page 17.** Oliver Wendell Holmes Jr., photograph, around 1859, Courtesy of Art & Visual Materials, Special Collections Department, Harvard Law School Library. **Page 18.** *Life at Harvard*. Color lithograph poster, Barbara Singer/Bridgeman Art Library. **Page 19.** *Hasty Pudding Flyer*. Color lithograph, June 19, 1860, The Harvard Theater Collection, The Houghton Library. Holmes played Sam in *Raising the Wind* and is listed on the program as "O.W. Holmes, Jr." **Page 21.** Oliver Wendell Holmes Jr., photograph, 1861, Courtesy of Art & Visual Materials, Special Collections Department, Harvard Law School Library. **Page 22.** Battle Flag of the Twentieth Massachusetts Regiment, silk, measures 60" x 69.5". Photograph courtesy of the President and Fellows of Harvard College. This is the display side. A replica of the flag is hanging in Memorial Hall at Harvard University. The original flag is now in an off-site, climate-controlled environment. **Page 23.** Letter from Oliver Wendell Holmes Jr. to His Mother. May 1861, courtesy of Special Collections Department, Harvard Law School Library. **Page 25.** "Field Hospital." Stereograph, 1862, © Collection of The New-York Historical Society. **Page 27.** Telegraph notifying Holmes's family of his injuries. Telegraph, 1862, Courtesy of Special Collections Department, Harvard Law School Library. **Pages 28–29.** Battlefield of Chancellorsville. Map, 1863, Jedediah Hotchkiss, Library of Congress Geography and Map Division. Shows troop positions and movements, roads, railroad, drainage, fords, and vegetation. Hotchkiss was a Confederate mapmaker who accompanied the troops. **Page 33.** Oliver Wendell Holmes's Diary. 1866. Courtesy of Special Collections Department, Harvard Law School Library. **Page 34.** Fanny Bowditch Dixwell. Photograph, 1860, Courtesy of Art & Visual Materials, Special Collections Department, Harvard Law School Library. **Page 36.** Oliver Wendell Holmes. Photograph, 1872, Courtesy of Art & Visual

Materials, Special Collections Department, Harvard Law School Library. **Page 37.** *The Common Law*, 1881. This book was written by Oliver Wendell Holmes Jr. and the notes in margin shown on this page were made by him in preparation of a lecture on the book. Courtesy of Special Collections Department, Harvard Law School Library. **Page 40.** Announcement of Holmes's Appointment. 1882, Courtesy of Special Collections Department, Harvard Law School Library. **Page 42.** Supreme Judicial Court of Massachusetts. photograph, circa 1899–1902, Courtesy of the Social Law Library, Boston. **Page 44.** The Holmeses' Summer Home in Beverly Farms, Massachusetts. Hand-colored photograph postcard 14 cm x 8.5 cm, circa 1910, Courtesy of the Beverly Public Library. **Page 47.** Holmes's *Commonwealth v. Perry* Dissent. 1891, courtesy of the Supreme Judicial Court, Archives and Records Preservation. **Page 49.** Strike at Carnegie's Steel Plant. Photomechanical print, 1892, G. A. Davis, from a sketch by C. Upham, Library of Congress Prints and Photographs Division. **Page 52.** Handkerchief Depicting Assassinated Presidents. Silk, 1901, © New-York Historical Society, New York, USA/Bridgeman Art Library. **Page 53.** Theodore Roosevelt. Photograph, 1903, Rockwood Photo Company, Library of Congress, Prints and Photographs Division. **Page 56.** Holmeses' House in Washington, D.C. Photograph, 1938, Harris & Irving Photos, Harris & Ewing/Collection of the Supreme Court of the United States. **Page 57.** *Edward Douglass White*. Painting, 1922, Albert Rosenthal, Collection of the Supreme Court of the United States. **Page 58.** Telegram from Roosevelt. 1903. Courtesy of Special Collections Department, Harvard Law School Library. **Page 60.** *A Glimpse of the Future— Fast and Tight*. Political Cartoon, circa 1890, North Wind Picture Archives. Depicts President Theodore Roosevelt attempting to "regulate the trusts by proper Government control." Appeared in the St. Paul (Minnesota) Pioneer Press. **Page 66.** Caricature of Holmes. 1909, Courtesy of Special Collections Department, Harvard Law School Library. **Page 74.** Children at Bibb Mill Textile Factory. Photographic print, 1909, Lewis Wickes Hines, Lewis Hine Photograph for the National Child Labor Committee, National Archives. Two boys standing on spinning frame to mend the broken threads or to put back the empty bobbins. **Page 81.** U.S. Supreme Court. Photograph, 1903, C. M. Bell, C. M. Bell/Collection of the Supreme Court of the United States. **Page 82.** Boston Common. Photograph, 1895, The Boston Athenaeum. **Page 85.** *Le Petit Parisien* announcing the assassination of Archduke Francis Ferdinand of Austria and his wife Sophie. Newspaper, June 29, 1914, Archives Charmet/Bridgeman Art Library. **Page 86.** Vladimir Lenin, circa 1917–1920, The Art Archive / Institute of Slavonic Studies / Marc Charmet. The Russian caption at the bottom of the poster reads, "The spectre that haunts Europe is Communism." **Page 90.** Holmes and Brandeis. Photograph, Collection of the Supreme Court of the United States. **Page 93.** Oliver Wendell Holmes. Painting, 1931, Charles Sidney Hopkinson, Collection of the Supreme Court of the United States. **Page 95.** Letter from Holmes to Pollock. 1929, Courtesy of Special Collections Department, Harvard Law School Library. **Page 97.** How His Successor Will Feel. 1932, Carl Rose, Courtesy of Special Collections Department, Harvard Law School Library.

Credits

Photo Credits

Cover (portrait), p. 42 courtesy of the Social Law Library, Boston; cover (background), pp. 63, 65, 74, 76 National Archives & Records Administration; pp. 4, 11, 12, 15, 17, 21, 34, 36 courtesy of Art & Visual Materials, Special Collections Department, Harvard Law School Library; p. 8 Lauros/Giraudon/Bridgeman Art Library; p. 9 © Hulton/Archive/Getty Images; p. 10 courtesy of the U.S. Naval Academy Museum; p. 18 Barbara Singer/Bridgeman Art Library; p. 19 The Harvard Theater Collection, The Houghton Library; p. 22 photograph courtesy of the President and Fellows of Harvard College; pp. 23, 27, 33, 37, 40, 58, 66, 95, 97 courtesy of Special Collections Department, Harvard Law School Library; p. 25 © Collection of The New-York Historical Society; pp. 28–29 Library of Congress Geography and Map Division; p. 44 courtesy of the Beverly Public Library; p. 47 courtesy of the Supreme Judicial Court, Archives and Records Preservation; p. 49 Library of Congress Prints and Photographs Division; p. 52 © New-York Historical Society, New York, USA/Bridgeman Art Library; p. 53 © Corbis; p. 56 Harris & Ewing/Collection of the Supreme Court of the United States; pp. 57, 67, 90, 93 Collection of the Supreme Court of the United States; p. 60 North Wind Picture Archives; p.71 Historical Society of Washington, D.C.; p. 81 C. M. Bell/Collection of the Supreme Court of the United States; p. 82 The Boston Athenaeum; p.85 Archives Charmet/Bridgeman Art Library; p. 86 The Art Archive/Institute of Slavonic Studies/Marc Charmet; p. 98 Wayne Wakeman.

Project Editors
Gillian Houghton, Jennifer Way

Series Design
Laura Murawski

Layout Design
Maria Melendez

Photo Researcher
Amy Feinberg

St. Patrick School
Washington, IL